OUR LONGING FOR ETERNITY

BY DONNA ALVES

I would like to give my appreciation to the owners of Biblehub.com for use of their on-line Bible verses used in this book.

A special and warmhearted thanks to Gayashan Elpitiya for his inspired illustrations.

ISBN: 069241231x

To my dearest friend, Susanne, whose tender friendship has been a wondrous gift from God to me.

CONTENTS

We can spend a lifetime looking for something or someone to satisfy the deepest longing of our heart. We search. We hope. We wait.

We may not even be aware of it, but we all have a longing for eternity in our hearts. So often, we find the answer to this longing in an unexpected place.

Journey with me through several intriguing life experiences; stories of challenges, hurts and healing, woven together with life-giving truths.

These will lead you to better understand what will satisfy the deepest longing of your heart.

1

A PLACE OF NO NEED

I was in a dark place, yet I was not afraid. I was alone and enclosed, yet felt no sense of fear. And though it seemed as if time did not exist, I realized that a moment had come. It was time for me to be born.

There was only one small problem: I didn't want to.

If you can imagine, I did not want to be born and I was very aware of it. I can remember it as though it were yesterday.

I was in a place where I was surrounded by peace; it was a perfect place filled with perfect peace. The environment in which I was resting was saturated with warmth and safety, more soothing than anything I have ever since felt in this life. I was immersed in tranquility. I was aware of what I felt. I felt no need. I had no wants. I was completely and fully satisfied; I lacked nothing.

All was perfect, until at an unexpected moment I felt an uncomfortable shift around me, a sort of tremor of something about to give way. I sensed a force of motion that I was being moved out from this perfect place of comfort. I was troubled. I was disturbed. I was quietly yet deeply alarmed.

This total completeness of peace, a peace beyond my understanding was, for the very first time, disrupted. I was shaken. Never before had I ever felt anything but safety. I became afraid.

Within moments I had a new awareness, a certain yet disturbing clarity, that the place I was moving toward was much different than the place I was now in. The place where I was headed was dark and cold, not filled with the peace and comfort I was so familiar with. Not at all. Although I was not sure of much, I was positive that this place I was headed towards was not like the place I was now. And I remember thinking to myself, at this very young age of zero, one precise thing:
"I don't want to go!"
And so I did what any young infant would do. I resisted. (Ha, no time for my stubbornness to develop—it was already in place!)

I Resisted

So, not yet being born, I began to put up a fight, saying exactly what was on my mind: "No." An adamant, "No, I don't want to go." (And you thought babies in utero couldn't talk!) I had not even made it down the birth canal yet, and there I was insisting on my way. (Not too strong-willed, right?) I fought, I squirmed, I wrestled, and did everything I could to stop myself from being moved toward this dark, cold place. I was determined that I was not leaving. I became more firm in my position and positively determined that I would not budge.
But then there came a moment of change. I sensed something. I paused. I hesitated. It was not really something I sensed, but more like... *someone*.

I remained still. I did not move.
Someone was there.
Not only was He there, but I knew He could see me.

**I remained still. I did not move. Someone was there.
Not only was He there, but I knew He could see me**

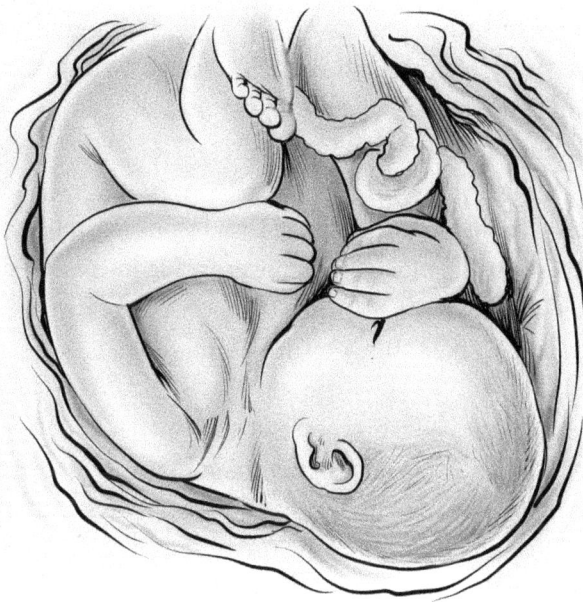

I froze. In that moment, I became fully aware that this
Someone was aware of my spiritual wrestling. He could
see me. And not only that, but He was aware of everything
I was thinking too. He was mindful of it all.

And so it was that He and I, without talking, just by
thinking, began conversing.

I understood His intentions toward me very clearly. He wanted me to go, to leave this place of comfort, and go out into this dark and cold place ahead of me.

I simply did not understand.

I again thought to myself, "But it's cold and dark and unsafe out there. Why would someone ask me to leave a wonderfully perfect safe place, perfect beyond description, and go out into a place so completely dark, cold, and unsafe? Why? Why would anyone ask such a thing of me?" I wondered. I pondered. I was confused. I did not say a word, but I just thought to myself.

I knew He was aware of what I was thinking. He knew my questions. He knew my concerns. He knew my fears. But He did not reply to any of these thoughts. Rather, He gently said to me, "But I want you to go."

This time, I replied a bit more softly, "But…. I don't want to go." I could not get out of my mind how this place that I was being asked to go to was filled with coldness and darkness. I just could not bear the thought of it. And, sweetly and gently, He said to me again, "But I want you to go." In that moment of time, a sense of something came over me. It was an awareness of my strong will being set against His. I could feel my resistance against Him.

I stayed still. I sensed what I was doing was not right. I could tell I had stepped over a line. So I stopped, and this time I listened.

And this time I heard Him ask me the same question, but

this time, I did not feel He was telling me that I had to go, but rather, *asking* me, "Will you go?"

I Was Touched By His Greatness

I sighed, at least inwardly. I was silent. Something had touched me in my emotions. I will never forget the way I felt that moment. It was that sense of Someone far greater than myself who had power over me to force me and impose His will on me. Yet He put His full power aside and chose to sensitively yield to me, and to be considerate of how I felt. I was completely humbled, yet honored. I was softened.

The situation had now taken a turn; and instead of Him asking me, I found myself gently asking Him, "You really want me to go?"
And He replied tenderly, "Yes, I want you to go."

Still bewildered, I replied, "But You know so well that I don't want to go."
And He softly and slowly, and even hesitantly answered, "I know."
It was strange. I sensed something more this time. It seemed as though as much as He really wanted me to go, that He Himself would be losing something, and that He was actually going to miss me. That even He Himself felt torn by my leaving this safe place. It touched me that He felt this way.
I felt His attachment toward me, His tenderness and empathy, and His compassion.

I felt His attachment toward me, His tenderness and empathy, and His compassion

I was so sure of the depth to which He was really feeling my struggle. He understood me, completely and absolutely. As I sensed this, I became more understanding of the depth to which He really cared about me, and that His asking me to leave was not because He didn't care, but just the opposite. It was because He *did* care, and that He wanted, even needed me, to go.

I began to have a change of heart. Yet, at the same time, I could feel the tears forming inside my unborn closed eyes. I so terribly and dreadfully did not want to go.

As I began to cry, another realization came to my mind that deepened my inner turmoil. I was now aware that, not only would I be losing my world of warmth, safety, and comfort, but I would be losing this amazing closeness with Him. I would be losing this pure intimacy with this special someone who knew me, who understood me, and completely loved me.

The thought of leaving was now worse than ever. Now my refusal to leave had plummeted from apprehension into sheer anguish.

My tears swelled and turned into weeping as I began thinking about His question to me.

I silently thought to myself:

"Will you go?" He had asked me so lovingly....

"Will you go?" He had asked me so gently....

"Will you go?" He asked as He yielded to me....

His deep sensitivity towards me so humbled me that all my resisting and fighting was gone. Yet I still did not understand *why*. Still nothing about my being asked to leave made any more sense to me now than it did when He asked me the first time.

But there was one thing that was different. One thing had changed.
I came to better understand Him, the One who was asking me to leave. He cared about me, and like a father, He was asking me to leave because He knew what was best. I now had a sense that it was not even an easy thing for Him to ask of me, but that He somehow knew much more than I, and His decision and His request was not just best for Him, but also best for me.
I hesitated. I held on. And with tears still in my eyes, I surrendered.

I Chose to Trust
I chose to trust, and even though I still did not understand, I let go, and finally replied to His question.
I said to Him, in between my tears, "Not my will, but Yours." And from within the womb, those were my very last words to Him.
So on that wintery day, with snow beginning to fall, I was born.
(See, I was right… Oh, baby, it was cold outside!)

This experience was engrained in my inner being and would shape my life forever. It would send me searching for that peace and love that I was once immersed in, for that relationship that I once knew, but had lost.
His indescribable love had left an invisible impression on my heart.

His indescribable love had left an invisible impression on my heart.

It would not be until my adult years that I would remember that He and I had this conversation or that I had known Him in this profoundly personal way. It was then I found out about the difficulties of my birth and how the doctors had such a hard time getting me out. Little did anyone know that during that time, I was battling, with all my little might, to stay in!

2

HE SEES

You may be saying to yourself, "Hmmm, that was quite an unusual story." I totally agree with you! But I also want to assure you the story is true. It is not something I made up *(it's too big a stretch for my imagination!).* You may be wondering how it's possible for anyone to remember something from before birth. "Isn't that impossible?" you ask. Almost impossible, but certainly, it would accurate to say it is very rare. This story was not something I remembered on my own, but rather it was revealed to me.

If you're skeptical and are asking questions such as, "What does this mean?" (Acts 2:13a), that's fine and I totally respect that. But please keep in mind, that this story was revealed not just for the purpose of comforting and encouraging me, but for your comfort and your encouragement, as well.

He Sees You

The same One who saw me also saw you. He saw you then as you lay cuddled up inside your mother's womb, and He sees you now. He wants you to hear these words from Him to you:

"I created your inmost being; I knit you together in your mother's womb. I watched you as you were being formed in utter seclusion, as you were woven together in the dark

of the womb. I saw you before you were born." (Psalm
139:13-15a)

The same One who saw me also saw you.

Just as I sensed in my story, He sees us while we are yet in
the womb. And He also knows about our lives right now,
and He tells us:
"Every day of your life was recorded in my book. Every
moment was laid out before a single day had passed."
(Psalm 139: 16)

Just as He knew me, He also knows you and is watching
over you. He knows everything about you: your feelings,
your questions, your doubts, your fears, and even your
future! You are so significant to Him that not only does
He know your name, but He tells you, "See, I have written
your name on the palms of my hands." (Isa. 49:16)

Who is this being who knows you so well? Who is He?
The only one who can know the thoughts of a person is
God. It is God who "knows the thoughts of man." (Ps
94:11a)
It is God who saw you while you were in the womb.
He Himself "formed you" and "knit you together."
The same hands of God that formed and "created the
heaven and the earth"
(Gen 1:1) were the same hands that formed you. He was
involved in your life even before you were born. Hear His
loving words to you right now:

"I know you. I know when you sit down and when you stand up. I understand your thoughts from far away. I see you when you travel and when you rest at home. I know everything you do. Before a word is on your tongue, I know it completely." (Ps 139:1-4)

He Cares About the Smallest Details

The Lord, He who is God, tells us Himself, "I the Lord search the heart and examine the mind." (Jeremiah 17:10a) God, just like a father, cares so much about us that He never takes His eyes off of us. He knows every single detail about us. And just so we don't miss the point of how even the insignificant details of our life matter to Him, He tells us, "Indeed, the very hairs of your head are all numbered." (Luke12:7)

Now, in my everyday life, keeping track of many things is very important, but knowing the number of hairs on my head is not one of them! Oh, and it's not just the total number of hairs that God knows; He has each one numbered, which indicates one specific number for each individual strand! Even more unnecessary! Do we get the point of how much God cares about us, even concerning the most insignificant details of our lives?

Oh, and just in case we miss the depth of care and love He has towards us by these facts, He also tells us, "precious are His thoughts about us." (Psalm 139:17a) His thoughts about us are not condemning, not critical, and not condescending; rather, they are precious, prized, and highly valued.

These thoughts about us are countless: "How vast is the sum of them, were I to count them, they would outnumber the grains of sand." (Psalm 139 v18) Can anyone count how many grains of sand there are? Well, while we're trying to come up with our best guesstimate, don't forget it's not just all the sand on the shorelines and beachfronts around the world, but it's all the grains underneath the ocean floor as well. Don't forget to count those too! In other words, His precious thoughts toward us are endless and impossible count!

His thoughts about us are not condemning, not critical, and not condescending; rather, they are precious, prized, and highly valued.

His Love Is Beyond Comprehension

Oh, "See what great love the Father has lavished on us…" (1 John 3:1a) If we could only begin to understand! But please don't try too hard to fathom His love, because He said His love toward us is so great that it "surpasses knowledge!" (Eph 3:19) His love is beyond our ability to imagine! So even if we think we understand how great God's love is toward us, we really have just begun to understand, because it's too great for our human minds to comprehend!

3

WHO HE IS

I know this whole idea of God being infinitely caring and loving may not be a view that everyone accepts. I am aware of this. There are many conclusions we come to on our own, and even more worldviews of who God is or is not. Some people may believe that God does not exist at all. Many people, whether believers or unbelievers, have questions, such as:

- If God exists, how could He allow innocent people to suffer?

- If He does exist, and has so much power, then why does He allow evil to exist?

- If God were so caring, why doesn't He do something about the injustices in this world?

Our Questions

Maybe the questions are more personal, and the person can't rationalize why God didn't spare them from the hurtful things that happened in their own personal life or to a loved one. Or the victims of world poverty or natural disasters—why doesn't God rescue them or answer their prayers? So many heartache-filled questions, so much tragedy and suffering.

It's better that we ask these hard questions rather than pretend they don't bother us. If we have questions about

Him, don't understand Him, or even if we are angry at Him, it's best we are transparent about it; besides, He can handle it. We might as well just tell Him, because He knows what we are thinking and feeling anyway!

After we wrestle, it is wise to pause and listen. Even as I wrestled and fought in the womb, fighting against God, questioning Him, not understanding His ways, once I sensed a glimpse of His greatness, I stopped. I sensed my smallness and my ignorance, and I had a change of heart. We too, need to consider His greatness and have a willingness to yield.

For no matter what we think about God, or what our view or conclusion is of who God is or is not, one important thing does not change:

What does not change is the fact of *who He is*.

God is God. Regardless of what we think or feel or conclude, He is who He says He is. None of our questions, doubts, hurts, anger, tantrums, or even our silent ignoring can do anything to change the fact of who He is.

God is God. Regardless of what we think or feel or conclude.

And all throughout history He has revealed Himself to those who have an open heart and mind to receive Him. It is possible for us to know who He is. The Bible tells us that if you want to know what God is like, we are to look at the Son. "The Son is the visible image of the invisible

God." (Col 1:15a)

God has revealed Himself through His Son, and through His inspired word. He has revealed Himself through people's personal experiences with Him as they spoke with Him, walked with Him, touched Him, and were healed and transformed by Him. Combining truths from God's book, the Bible, along with many of these testimonies, following is a brief description of "Who God is."

Who God Is

God is… always there for you.
When you call to Him, He hears you,
God is not deaf; He made the ear!

He is not unjust or uncaring.
Though He allows hurt and pain,
He is not indifferent to your suffering.

Though life may seem unfair, there is no unfairness in Him;
He has no wrong intent or wrong motives.
He does not have a critical attitude,
Not toward you or anyone.

Though life may seem unfair, there is no unfairness in Him;

He can identify with you,
And He does care.

He sent His Spirit to comfort you.

He allowed free will,
Because love gives us a choice;
Love does not force.

He allowed free will, because love gives us a choice; love gives us a choice, love does not force.

He chose to allow evil to exist,
For He saw it was best;
Even if we don't understand.
His ways are higher than ours.

What He does is never wrong.
He does not change.
He never betrays.

He is never apathetic,
He is never indifferent towards you.
He may lovingly correct you,
But He never rejects you.

He did not wait for us to "get our act together";
He loved us first.
And while we were yet sinners, He gave His Son
To die in our place.
There is only way to the Father,
And that is through the Son,
Jesus Christ, Who is the visible image

WHO HE IS   19

Of the invisible God.
Fully God; fully man.

His love for us is not based on our performance,
He loved us before the foundation of the world was laid.
Christ gave up His own life for us, even though we didn't deserve it.
His love toward us does not change, even when we fall short.
When you feel He is not aware of what is going on in your life,
Remember He who made the eye can see!

He never abandons you
And He never forsakes you;
Even though it may feel He does.

He is always just.
He is giving,
He is merciful,
He is truthful,
He is patient,
He is kind.
He is good.

"There is no wickedness in Him." (Ps 92:15)
In Him there is no darkness at all. (1 John 1:5)

This is the truth about Who God is.

His Invitation to You

This is the God who really cares about you—enough to die for you.

You can choose to believe in Him right this moment. You can receive Him into your life by simply asking, "Lord, come into my life, forgive me of my sins."

If you decide to ask Christ into your life, wonderful things will begin to happen!

4

BELIEF

It is so wonderfully simple:
We all need love. "God is Love." (1 John 4:8b) Therefore, we all need God.

We all need love. "God is Love." (1 John 4:8b) Therefore, we all need God.

From the very beginning, this is how it was intended it to be.
God designed every person to need love. Every person not only needs love, but more specifically, needs God's love.

Not only are we designed to need His love, but also, to need Him. In order to receive His love, we need to have a relationship with Him. It is built-in to every one of us to have a need for a relationship with Him, through Christ His Son; to be loved by Him and to belong to Him, to be His child. God has the heart of a loving dad. He is the perfect dad. And He wants to be our dad.
In short, we all need love, we all need a dad, and we all need God.

Perhaps all of this makes sense to you, but yet, you still have questions. Many times we want to believe but still have areas of unbelief. This is not unusual. Both believers and non-believers struggle with this. Did you know it is possible for people to have both belief and unbelief at the same time? An illustration of this is a real story about a very honest dad who had a son who since childhood suffered from seizures and convulsions. At times the boy was thrown into a fire and he would get severely burned. As he convulsed, he was thrown into water and would almost drown. In desperation, the dad brought His son to Jesus, pleading for help, and saying, "But if You can do anything, take pity on us and help us." (Mark 9:21) Jesus replied, "If you can? All things are possible to him who believes." (v23)

Without a hesitation, "Immediately the boy's father cried out and said, "I do believe; help my unbelief."

Help My Unbelief

We can say the same thing when we know we need help, but still have so many questions; we can say, "Lord, I believe, please help my unbelief." And God will help us with any unbelief we have.

Jesus prayed for the man's son. At first, the boy became so much like a corpse that most of the people in the crowd said, "He is dead!" (v26.) But Jesus took him by the hand and raised him, and he got up." (V27) In spite of the boy's father having both belief and unbelief, the boy was healed.

At times we struggle to believe. In our heart we feel we want to believe, but in our minds we think differently. This "tug-of-war within" is a conflict between our hearts and our minds. Our minds are carnal, having an argumentative and hostile attitude toward God. Did you know that our human thinking, the carnal mind, is even filled with hatred towards God? We are told, "our carnal mind, our sinful nature, is always hostile toward God." (Rom 8:7) This explains to us that we should follow our heart, and not allow any disbelief in our mind to stand in our way. "If today you hear His voice, harden not your heart."(Heb. 3:15)

Just a word of caution, if you please:
In this area of disbelief, we need to tread carefully, being careful that we do not cross over the line and become disrespectful of who God is. We must be humble and mindful that He is the Creator and we are the creation; we are but dust. "For He knows how we are formed, He remembers that we are dust. (Ps 103:14) "But who are you, a mere man, to talk back to God? Will what is formed say to the One who formed it, 'Why did you make me like this?'" (Rom. 9:20) "Who are you, a mere human being, to argue with God?"

So yes, it is understandable and human that we wrestle with unbelief, but we must be respectful of the fact that whether we believe God or not, that our opinion does not change the truth: He still is the holy and all-powerful God.

God Understands Our Questions

Just as the boy's father did, you too can choose to believe. God understands our struggles and doubts. He sees and knows the sincerity of our hearts.

He says, "You will seek Me, and you will find Me when you seek Me with all your heart." (Jer. 29:13)

Don't allow disbelief to stand in your way of embracing the Father that you and every person so desperately needs. He will receive you just as you are—questions, problems and all. It doesn't matter how far from God you may feel you are. It doesn't even matter how messed up your life may be. "He will give a crown of beauty for ashes." (Is. 61:3) God's specialty is making beauty out of ashes!

Admitting Our Need

So often we don't turn to God until we feel we need Him. This was the case of a young man who irresponsibly spent everything he had. It wasn't until he reached the point where he began to "be in need," (Luke 15:14b) that he returned to his father. When the young man "came to his senses" (v17) he decided to set out and go back to his father to tell his dad:

"'Father, I have sinned against heaven and against You. I am no longer worthy to be called your son,' (v18a) and, 'Make me like one of your hired servants.' So he got up and went to his father." (v20)

Just as this son admitted his need, his mistakes and his unworthiness, so too, we need to admit these same three things. As we come to the Father, we are to:

- Admit our need for Him,
- Confess our sins, and
- Humble ourselves.

There was a beautiful ending to this story:
"But while he was still a long way off, his father saw him and was filled with compassion for him; he ran to his son, threw his arms around him and kissed him." (Luke 15:20)
In the same way, our heavenly Father waits for us to come home.
The Father is there, waiting with open arms to receive us.

The Father is there, waiting with open arms to receive us.

When He sees us, he does not just stand there, he runs to us. He runs to meet us and says, "Let's have a feast and celebrate. For this son of mine was dead and is alive again; he was lost and is found. So they began to celebrate." (v23b,24)

This son, who was irresponsible and prideful and "squandered his wealth in wild living," (v13) was now accepted home by the father. And although we may not be irresponsible or be exactly like this wild, rebellious son, we also fall short in any ways.
Even if we feel we are a good person, we are not perfect.

We All Fall Short
We all have faults and flaws, and at times do wrong. We all make mistakes.

It is a fact: we all live in a state of sin.
"For all have sinned and fall short of the glory of God."
(Rom. 3:23) Everyone falls short; and that includes every
person ever born. "If we say that we have never sinned,
we make God a liar and His word has no place in us." (1
John 1:10)

And, "If we claim to be without sin; we deceive ourselves
and the truth is not in us."(1 John 1:8) "For the wages of
sin is death, but the gift of God is eternal life in Christ
Jesus our Lord." (Rom. 6:23)

It doesn't matter how "good" a person we are. We are not
saved by what we have done, nor by our good deeds. We
are saved by God's grace through faith, lest anyone might
boast. "For it is by grace you have been saved, through
faith; and this is not from yourselves, it is the gift of God."
(Eph. 2:8)

It is God the Father's desire for everyone to have eternal life
and to have a personal relationship with Him through Christ.
For God so loved you and me (and everyone in the world)
that "He gave His only Son that whosoever believes in Him,
would not perish but have everlasting life." (John 3:16)

5

FATHER APPROVAL

Everyone needs a dad. It is a universal need for every person around the world.

In this relationship with our dad, there is a small factor that has a big impact on every one of us; that is, our father's feelings towards us and His opinion of us.

Our Father's Opinion of Us

How our father feels about us and His opinion of us is of huge significance in our lives.

How our father feels about us and His opinion of us is of huge significance in our lives.

I did not realize just how significant until someone asked me, "Are you looking for your parent's approval?"

Was I? Are you? And if we are, is that ok? If we are looking for our father's, or our parent's approval, is this pointing to a problem?

I began to ask myself questions such as, "Was I suffering from approval addiction, where I could not feel good about myself apart from my parent's approval of me? Is it normal and healthy to want approval from our parents, particularly our dad or whoever is the father figure in our lives?"

With these questions I mind, I decided to go to a most reliable source for my answer; to words that "are alive," (Heb. 4:12a) the Word of God.

"For the word of God is alive and active. Sharper than any double-edged sword, it penetrates even to dividing soul and spirit, joints and marrow; it judges the thoughts and attitudes of the heart." (Heb. 4:12)

So I began to read, and sure enough, in the midst of a story, I found the answer: People were coming to John, and among those people was Jesus, who also came to be baptized by John. And "as soon as Jesus was baptized, and He came up out of the water, at that very moment the heaven was opened, and He saw the Spirit of God descending like a dove and lighting on Him, and a voice from heaven spoke." (Matt 3:16)

A voice, God the Father, was about to speak. What would this Father have to say about His Son? This was a paramount moment for His Son, who was now stepping into His Divine Ministry. What announcement would the Father make about His Only Son, who on this the day was about to embark upon His mission to save the entire world? What proclamation would the Father choose? This moment was huge.

Perhaps the Father would chose to declare to all that His Son was the One Who was chosen to save all mankind from eternal death; or perhaps He would explain how His Son was the One Who was with Him before time existed and had formed the universe with His own hands. "Through Him (the Son) all things were made; without Him nothing was made that has been made." (John 1:3)

Or would the Father want to declare the power and greatness of Christ, His supremacy and authority? Would He declare to everyone how every knee will bow to Him who is the King of Kings? "King of Kings and Lord of Lords." (Rev. 19:16b)
Would the Father speak for several minutes, or go on for hours?
And then the Father's voice was heard, and He spoke saying: "This is my Son, whom I love; with Him I am well pleased." (Matt 3:17)

The Father Approves of His Son

One sentence. That was it. One powerful, tender, love-filled message.

The Father, openly and publicly, revealed His heart towards His Son.

It was deep and it was personal. He spoke about how He felt.

The Father revealed how He felt in His heart towards His "One and Only Son… He loved His Son. He approved of His Son. He was pleased with His Son… His one and only boy."

(I use this word "boy" will full respect. I use it to emphasize how God is a real dad who loves His Son as an earthly dad loves his son… his boy. Father and Son.)

The Father gave no long speech. (So often what the Father says to us is short but so overwhelmingly and incredibly powerful!) He is speaking; can we hear Him?

Most often His voice is not found in whirling winds, crashing earthquakes, or in booming thunder. Hear how He speaks:

"Then a great and powerful wind tore the mountains apart and shattered the rocks before the Lord, but the Lord was not in the wind. After the wind there was an earthquake, but the Lord was not in the earthquake. After the earthquake came a fire, but the Lord was not in the fire. And after the fire came a gentle whisper." (1 Kings 19:11-12)

Most often His voice is not found in whirling winds, crashing earthquakes, or in booming thunder.

He speaks to us simply, powerfully and gently, in His still small voice. The Father proclaimed the love and bond He had with His Son.

He shared how He valued His Son.

It's OK to Need Our Father's Approval

After reading this story where God the Father formally announced His approval of His Son, I was at peace in concluding that this was an example of how we, too, need our Father's approval; and that it is perfectly healthy and normal to desire and long for approval from our father and from our parents.

I accepted that I had a need for approval and acceptance from my father.

I was comforted to know that this was a genuine need and perfectly normal.

Wouldn't it be so refreshing if each one of our dads said to us how they are content, satisfied, and pleased with us? How wonderful we would feel to hear our earthly father tell us that we bring him great joy, and that he delights in us, that we make him happy and that he is proud of us. That we make him smile! Certainly this is something everybody in the world desires and needs.

Ways the Father Loves Us

I looked at the story again, this time appreciating a few more things about the ways in which God the Father loves us:

1. What the Father did not say He spoke not about what the Son *does*, but about *who the Son was*. He spoke not about what the Son was *going to do* but rather about *who the Son was*.

He spoke not about what the Son does, but about who the Son was.

Not that what Christ did or would do was being minimized, in any way, but the Father's supreme importance was focused on the love He had for His Son, apart from the great things the Son had already done and was yet to do. This is how the Father loves us. His heart toward us is focused primarily on one thing: us, and our belonging to Him.

Our Father's center of attention toward us in on our belonging to Him; and it is focused on our *being*, not on our *doing*.

Our Father's center of attention toward us in on our belonging to Him; and it is focused on our being, not on our doing.

Imagine yourself as a newborn baby, your father looking at you and holding you as his heart overflows with love for you.

He loves you… just because.

He loves you not because you have done anything. (Ok, you were born, but that did not take a lot of effort on your part.) Your dad is there and he loves you just because you are his. You are a part of him. You belong to him.

And this love from the Father is the same for us. His love for us is not based on what we do, or about who we are, or on who or what we become.
His love for us is given freely, like a gift is given, without any strings attached. Much the same way, we are offered His gift of eternal life.
It is a gift that we did not and cannot earn or merit; not by our own doing and not in our own strength. "For it is by grace you have been saved, through faith—and this is not from yourselves, it is the gift of God— not by works, so that no one can boast." (Eph. 2:8-9)

Not to misunderstand that this unconditional love from God implies that we have the liberty to do what is wrong or that it exempts us from doing the things that are right and what we are responsible to do. We are not to take advantage of the grace of God or His mercy or His kindness, as this would not be loving on our part.
We are to do good works and to "be about our Father's business." Actually, that is one reason why we were created. We were created to do good works.

"For we are God's handiwork, created in Christ Jesus to do good works, which God prepared in advance for us to do. (Eph 2:10)
And others are to see these good works. "Let your light shine before men in such a way that they may see your good works, and glorify your Father who is in heaven."

(Matt. 5:16)

So, from the words the Father chose not to speak, we can know that His love for us in not based on our performance or on our doing.

His love poured out onto us is unconditional and unending.

His love poured out onto us is unconditional and unending.

---

2. The Father did not speak about what the Son would mean to all those lives He would touch, heal, and save. Instead, the Father's focus was on the bond of their relationship; everything focused on the Father-Son relationship. This reminds us that no matter how important our life mission or "our ministry" is, our relationship with God is to remain first and foremost. We are to always remember and never forget God, our "First Love." He is very jealous about our keeping Him first.

"But I have this against you, that you have left your first love." (Rev.2:4)

This is what is of most importance to God. You. You and Him.

3. We can extract from this story some sweet examples and a model of what an earthly father, a parent, a father figure, or caregiver's love toward us was intended to look like:

- An earthly father is to be there for us.

- Our dad is to be present, not absent *(especially at*

special events).

- Our dad needs to speak tenderly to us.
- His words toward us are to be affirming words.
- It is appropriate that our dad speaks well of us and praises us in public.
- As the dove touched the Son, our dad is to be engaged with us.
- The Father said He was pleased with His Son, and so our earthly dad is to share how he feels toward us and reveal his emotions to us.
- We are to feel our father's heart and emotions toward us.
- As God the Father said "this is my Son," we too need to feel the love of belonging to our dad. That our dad is proud to call us his own.
- We are to feel our dad's acceptance of us.
- We are to feel attached, not detached, that we are his child whom he loves.
- As the Heavenly Father was well-pleased with the Son, so we also long for the approval from our earthly father.

We all long for the approval from our parents and especially from our earthly father. When we have this in our lives, there is a satisfaction and confidence that emanates in our lives.

And so based on the words the Father spoke from heaven that day, we can better describe how God loves us.
He loves us because we belong to Him.

But what about those many people who have not had the privilege to experience this sort of fatherly love in their lives? For so many people, both men and woman alike, there is a gap, sometimes more like a chasm, due to the absence of the father's love in their lives.

For those who have had to live without the love of their father in their lives, the result is deprivation. Deprivation leaves a person hungry, sometimes starving for the love of a father they never had. This absence of the father's love causes many sorts of consequences in a person' life.
This is why our understanding and receiving love from our Heavenly Father is so critical.

Man is imperfect; man can—and will—fail us. Sadly, many dads fail their sons and daughters. Even the most seemingly perfect dad can disappoint their child or fail them at some point or in one important area or their lives. Surely having a good father helps, but even having a good father is not enough. This is because a dad is imperfect, he is human, and he makes mistakes. Though our dads may have tried their best, they will, in one way or another, fall short.

The Missing Dad

So what about the dad who was really *not* there? If your dad was missing, or even one of your parents was absent in your life, you may find just reading this topic annoying and even a bit irritating. You may be thinking, "My dad, my mom, they were never really there for me. They hardly ever paid any attention to me. Even now, they barely know me."

That is so sad. Perhaps your dad left you. Maybe he left but came back and now you have re-connected with him. Perhaps he was there for you, but only when you were a young child; and then when you became an adult, he didn't know how to be there for you to give you guidance and support. Maybe he had to leave on military duty, or his profession often caused him to be frequently out of town. Maybe he had to work several jobs. Maybe he had no jobs at all. Sadly, fathers can be absent or distance for many other reasons; they can be missing due death, disease, or divorce. It can be from his being an alcoholic or in prison. Sometimes a father simply "checks out" because of his own issues of his past where he was once deprived of the love and support he needed from his parents, particularly, his dad.

And so the cycle continues.

Each person will have their own particular situation where they felt their dad was missing.

The Impact of the Missing Dad

No matter what the reason, the absence of a father has a significant impact on a person's life. It will significantly affect how they view other people throughout their life. For women, there will be a main impact on her view and expectations towards men throughout her lifetime. For men, they usually have a harder time acting like men and are less equipped to be husbands and fathers.

In both men and women who are not raised by committed

and faithful fathers, they are more likely to lack confidence, lack self-control, lack kindness, and lack a sense of responsibility.

Whatever the cause of the father not being there, this separation and lack of relationship is difficult for both the parent and children. It is a strain on the extended family, too.

What is your personal situation?
What kind of father do you have, or did you have?
Maybe your dad left you.
Maybe he didn't physically leave you, but you feel like he is not there for you.
Maybe he died unexpectedly and you never got a chance to tell him things that were on your mind, whether good or bad.
Maybe your dad is alive but you never see him and he never calls you; he treats you as though you don't even exist.
Maybe there are a lot of unresolved issues between you and your dad.
Maybe you have tried over and over to connect with your dad only to be disappointed one more time. Now you have given up.
Maybe you sense your dad is mad at you and you're not even sure as to the reason why.

There is nothing in this temporal world that is "big" enough, "deep" enough "or lasts long enough" to fill the "forever" in our hearts.

Maybe your dad is in your life and you wish he wasn't!
Maybe years have passed and you have convinced yourself
that it was so long ago, there is no need to revisit the past,
since there is nothing you can do about it anyway. You have
concluded it is easier to ignore the hurt and bury the pain.
Maybe you are so upset about how your dad has not treated
you right that you are mad at him, and over time, your
respect for him has so dwindled that you have even have
grown to hate him.
Maybe you are at the point that even the word "dad" causes
you to cringe.
Maybe you are done, you are so fed up with this father
issue being such a sore spot in your life that you have
adapted the "I couldn't care less" attitude in an attempt
to compensate for your loss... the loss of your dad.
Some of you may have been physically and or emotionally
abandoned, not just by your dad, but by your mom as well.
From this rejection of both your parents, you feel a hole in
your life so deep that it feels as though it has no bottom.

Parental Rejection

Parental rejection is one of the most severe rejections a
person can suffer in life. It is one of the deepest losses we
can suffer.

It is important to guard our hearts. "Above all else, guard
your heart, for everything you do flows from it." (Prov.
4:23) While it is our desire to be approved by our parents
or by people, and to be accepted by them, we cannot
put our complete trust in our parents. It is not safe to

trust people to find our worth and value, for people are imperfect and therefore can so easily, and many times unintentionally, fail us.

That is why it is best that we look for our approval and to find our identity and value from our Heavenly Father. Not that we can't put some confidence in people (in men), but it is better to put our trust in God.

"It is better to trust in the Lord than to put confidence in man." (Ps.118:8)
Our desire for approval from people cannot be based on our need to please people. Our focus needs to be on pleasing God.

This statement is not a contradiction to the fact it is normal and healthy to need acceptance from our earthly father. Rather, it is an additional principle: We are not to get caught up in winning the approval of our dad—not our dad, not our mom, not our friends, not of any person. We are not to supposed try To win the approval of other people.

Paul explains how his focus was to please God rather than people: "Am I now trying to win the approval of human beings, or of God? Or am I trying to please people? If I were still trying to please people, I would not be a servant of Christ." (Gal 1:10) And again Paul encourages us not to please man, but to please God: "But just as we have been approved by God to be entrusted with the gospel, so we speak, not to please man, but to please God who tests

FATHER APPROVAL   41

our hearts. (1 Thess. 2:24)

And to be sure we understand the importance of keeping these priorities in proper perspective, Jesus makes this strong statement: "If you love your father or mother more than you love me, you are not worthy of being mine; or if you love your son or daughter more than me, you are not worthy of being mine." (Matt. 10:37)

It Is Better to Trust in God

Yes, desiring our father and our parent's approval is healthy and normal, but at the same time, it is better to trust in God for His approval.

"It is better to trust in the Lord than to put confidence in man," or in a broader sense, we should not to make it our aim to seek approval from any person, not father, mother, father figure, an authority figure, a famous figure, a boss, a spouse, not even friends; but rather, our goal is to receive the approval from God.

For those people whose parents have failed you,
disappointed you,
    disregarded you,
        hurt you, and
            abandoned you... God has a word to bring you comfort:

He wants you to know that His heart breaks for you and with you. He wants you to know that He sees you... as an orphan.

He understands your aloneness and that He can identify with your feeling rejected.

And He promises to be there for you.
"He is a Father to the fatherless." (Ps: 68:5)
"He is a Father of orphans, champion of widows, is God in his holy house." (Ps:68:5)

And even if you feel you have been abandoned by God, in actuality, you have not been forsaken or abandoned by Him. "Though my father and mother forsake me, the Lord will receive me." (Ps. 27:10)
"Even if my father and mother abandon me, the Lord will hold me close." (Ps. 27:10)
"For my father and my mother have left me, and the Lord has taken me up." (Ps. 27:10)
God never leaves us nor forsakes you:
"For the Lord your God goes with you; He will never leave you nor forsake you," (Deut. 31:6b) even though in our mind we may think he has.
We must trust Him, for He does not lie. "God, Who never lies." (Titus 1:2b)

If He says He is there for us, then He is, whether it appears so or not. Whether it feels like or not.

To Whom Else Can We Turn?

Besides, if our very own parents forsake us and reject us, to whom else can we go? If our very own parents do not receive us, who else will?
Even when we even feel like running away from God, we must ask ourselves, "Who else is there to run to?"
To whom else can we turn to heal us and love us?

To whom else shall we go?

As Jesus was speaking to a crowd, "At this point many of his disciples turned away and deserted Him." (John 6:66) Then Jesus turned to the Twelve and asked, "Are you also going to leave?" Simon Peter answered Him, "Lord, to whom shall we go? You have the words of eternal life." (John 6: 67-68)

To whom else can we look to? There is no one else who knows us and cares for us as Our Heavenly Father.

We may be confused and feel forsaken by God, we may even feel abandoned by God, but we must put our feelings aside and embrace the truth. The truth is that God loves us and receives as His own.

He is there to love us and comfort us. He accepts us just as we are and will love us back to emotional health. He will love us back to life!

He is your refuge: "God is our refuge and strength, a very present help in trouble." (Ps 46:1)

He is your hiding place: "You are my hiding place; You will protect me from trouble and surround me with songs of deliverance." (Ps. 32:7)

He is your hiding place and your protector: "Keep me as the apple of your eye; hide me in the shadow of your wings." (Ps 17:8)

It hurts when our dads or our parents are not there for us; our relationship with our dads is something that is irreplaceable. And when the relationship is bad or simply non-existent, we feel a pain deep inside.

We feel alone and hurt.

That is why we can be so thankful for who God is because He is our Heavenly Father who is there to help us pick up and to help piece back together all the broken pieces in our lives.

He is a Perfect Father who never fails us.

He is a Perfect Father who never leaves us or forsakes us.

He is perfect and His love towards us is perfect.

So if and when our earthly father, or father figure in our lives, fall short, we have the love of our Heavenly Father that assures us of our worth and value.

The Heavenly Father wants to be a part of our life. He wants to have a relationship with us. He asks us to "draw near to Him, He will draw near to you..." (James 4:8a) "The Lord is near to all who call on Him, to all who call on Him in truth." (Ps 145:18)

He stands with His arms open wide and "He calls you by your name" (Isaiah 45:4b)

Will you embrace Him as your Dad? Will you open your heart to Him?

And if you already have a relationship with Your Heavenly Father, will you ask Him to draw you closer to Him?

He loves you more than you can know.

6

WE ALL HAVE NEEDS

It is the cry of our heart to have a love connection and to have a bond not just with God, but with also with one another.
The need for love and the need to have relationships with others is how God made us. We were all made to long for closeness, to need nurturing and to desire intimacy.

This healthy love connection with others, not only satisfies us but it is also what motivates us.

This healthy love-connection with others, not only satisfies us, but it is also what motivates us

---

This unique connection spurs us on to give, to love, and to live. This connection is filled with healthy longings to be close and intimate. These desires are essential to life and are so worth celebrating! Unless, that is, you have been critically wounded by them! In that case, the celebrating ceases and quickly turns into sadness. I found this out through my own life experience, for in my life, the love-connection was missing. People have many ways of dealing with the absence of this love connection. This is a story of how I handled it in my life:

When the Love Connection Is Missing

I was one of those kids who looks happy on the outside but who was really dying on the inside. There was a part of me that was very happy, yet at the same time a part of me was also very sad. My basic physical needs were met, but my emotional needs were not. Not only were they not met, but over the years the wounds of emotional neglect and abuse kept growing deeper and deeper. I was an upbeat kid with a positive attitude, so I just figured, "Hey, I'm not gonna let this get me down. I'm tough; I can handle this on my own, thank you very much!"

So I made a decision to handle my hurts by being strong. Since all the abuse, rejection, disappointment, misunderstandings, and pain were too much for me to deal with, I decided I would have no needs in my life. I figured I would do myself a big favor and prevent myself from suffering by having no needs. So I set up the walls, nice and high, figuring the problems and pain would eventually work themselves out. I got very busy teaching myself how to survive. Over time I perfected my "emotional survival skills" by refusing to allow myself to be wounded by lack of any emotional needs. I chose to handle my hurts in a way that is called "repression."

I Chose Repression

I got busy enjoying achievements and scholastics while I learned how not to hurt, how not to need, and how not to cry. I was tough. I was strong. Things were working out relatively nicely until I became so skilled at teaching myself how not to need that I ended up teaching myself how not to feel! Oh no! I had numbed myself to such an extreme that I had lost touch with my own emotions.

So much for my brilliant plan! In the process of my learning how to survive, I had totally lost touch with my own feelings and my own self. I found myself in a very deep mental and emotional crisis.

People say in times of crisis and difficulty we respond by either drawing closer to God or pushing Him away. At the time when I was so wounded, I was not even aware of how I was responding to God, I was just doing what I needed to do to survive. I knew about God, but I really didn't know who He was. I would go to church, trying to understand how God fit into my life, but He always seemed so far away. I was trying to draw closer to God, but I did not know how.

So, there I was. I had shut myself down to the point where I became numb; I was deadened to almost everything... except one thing:
The gnawing pain that reminded me, everyday, how hurting and empty I was.
I thought that all my pain would eventually work itself *out*, only to find out that all the pain had worked itself *in*. And the pain was now deep inside me and beyond my ability to bear

A Need for God

It was then that a need for God began to surface. And it was need that I could not ignore. And that is where God found me.
Numb. Broken. Alone. Confused.

He called to me in His quiet-still-soft-voice and let me know He was there to help me.
I responded. I surrendered to Him. This was my moment of change and what inspired and marked the season of hope in my life. Later on, I would come to find out that this experience was called being "born again."
In my place of deep inner pain, with no person able to help me, that was my only solution... to fall on my knees, helpless, and beg God to pick me up.

God encourages us to come to Him: "Humble yourself before the Lord and He will lift you up." (James 4:10) He lifted me up.

That is exactly what He did.

Life happens. And when we don't know how to handle something, it is so easy to numb ourselves without realizing it. We do it to survive. But there comes a point where it just doesn't work anymore. It is a terrible feeling to sincerely want to share your heart, but you can't, because you don't even know how you feel in your own heart!

We all have a need to share our hearts. We also have many other needs. We can deny them or try to ignore them, as I tried to. A severe consequence of this denial process is that it keeps us from authenticity, causing us to remain strangers to ourselves, being unaware of own true feelings and needs.

Denying our feelings or needs only results in hurting ourselves and others, and it does not change the fact that our needs will still be there.

Denying our feelings or needs only results in hurting ourselves and others.

A Three-Part Being

The truth is that every person is a three-part being, and everybody has the same basic needs:

- A physical need for air, water, food and rest,
- Emotional needs, such as being loved and accepted, and
- A spiritual need to know God personally, and understand His true identity.

What would happen to a person who did not have their physical need of drinking enough water met over a long period of time? There would be symptoms of dehydration, which if let untreated would cause consequences; and if deprived long enough, could even cause physical death. Similarly, if emotional or spirituals needs are not met, over a long period of time, there will be symptoms as well— symptoms such as sadness, anxiety, worry, increase of fears, depression, loss of hope.

Just as in the case with our bodies physically, so emotionally and spiritually we can also "die" from not having our needs met over a long period of time.

And that is exactly what happened to me. I did not want to admit it, and I fought it as best and as long as I could, but the truth was that my unmet emotional and spiritual needs caused severe consequences in my life, and brought me to a the end of myself, almost to the point of death. (Now that is serious!)

Unmet emotional and spiritual needs can cause severe consequences in our lives.

Had God not reached out to me, I would not be here to tell the story. I had no idea of the lies that had crept into

my life, especially guilt, shame, and condemnation.
I reached a breaking point, and God rescued me. I surrendered my life to Christ and began a new season of my
life filled with freedom and healing.

A Correct View of God

However, there was one more huge piece in the area of
my spiritual needs that had not been met. I didn't know
it was missing, but one the weekend, on just an ordinary
day, I was about to find out.

I was happily singing along one day in my apartment,
going about my everyday routine. I was now in my twen-
ties and my life finally seemed to be going along, at least
for a while, without any major crisis.

There I was singing merrily, repeating a chorus to a song
that had the lyrics, "Lord, You have been good," when I
was suddenly and abruptly interrupted.
It was not a knock at the door, but rather, it was Someone
who spoke. "You don't believe that," He said.
I replied, "Huh?" I was caught off guard and so taken back
by the suddenness and authority of the disruption. Then
I thought to myself, "What did He say?" After recovering
from the shock of what God said, I questioned myself. "I
don't? I don't believe that God is good?" I paused. I sat. I
thought about what He had said. And I thought to myself,
but I was not ungrateful. To the contrary, I was so thankful and appreciative for all the good things He had done
in my life, how could I not think He was good? But He

said I didn't think He was good, and He was very sure of it from the tone in which He spoke to me. So, I sat and thought; and in quietness, I reflected.

Then, I became saddened. Thoughts of the many deep hurts in my life began to surface; times when I had felt abandoned, rejected, and alone.

Slowly I began to realize that during these times I had come to a conclusion about God.

I had concluded that God did *not* care.

I thought I was just hurt, when in fact, I was not. The truth was that I was mad at God for leaving me to suffer alone. I had concluded that God was absent and indifferent in my darkest hours. (Sigh.)

I now realized how right He was. Now I was aware how I had falsely accused Him of not caring and of not being good. And I began to think about how I had arrived at this conclusion. Without my being aware, my line of thinking had gone something like this:

I did not believe God had my best interest in mind, because He allowed me to suffer.

Since He had allowed me to suffer, this implied He wasn't that concerned about me.

I knew this because despite His having the ability to rescue me, He did not, which would imply that He didn't care enough about me.

Then I obviously didn't matter enough to Him; and if I didn't matter enough, He must not think I was that important to Him.

And if I were not important, than how could He really care about me?

And if He didn't really care, then He can't be kind.
And if He's not kind, then He must mean.
And if mean, then bad.
The opposite of bad being good,
Therefore, He can't be good.
And so, without my intentionally wanting to be angry
at God,
I had concluded that…
God was not good.

It was really hard to receive that word of correction from
God, but I knew it was for my benefit. Such an important
insight can be gained from this story, and it is this:

If we have a wrong image of God, our spiritual needs
cannot fully be met.

**If we have a wrong image of God, our spiritual needs
cannot fully be met.**

We may come to know Him through a personal relationship with Jesus Christ, and so our spiritual needs are met
when we are "born anew." However, if we are doubtful
of His character, and do not have a correct view of Who
God is, we will always keep a certain part of ourselves
closed off to Him.
So, in order for our spiritual thirst to be fully quenched,
we not only need to have a personal relationship with Him,
but in addition, we need to have a right understanding of
His true identity.

We need a correct view of God and His upright character.
We must believe that He is good.

If we are suspicious of God in any way, if we have a wrong
conclusion of who God is, if we have doubt that He is all,
good, fair, just, kind, merciful, and caring, then we will
not be able to fully embrace Him.
And if we keep Him at arms' length, our spiritual needs
will never be fully met.

7

SPIRITUAL NEEDS

Our physical needs are obvious and our emotional needs are also quite noticeable; but our spiritual needs are often not so apparent. Our spiritual needs may go fairly unnoticed, until, at some point in our lives, we find ourselves in a difficult situation. It is at this point that we find ourselves crying out to God in desperation, very much aware of our spiritual needs and our need for God. For some people this may not happen until their grown-up years, but for others it may happen earlier. There may be many different times throughout our lives when we become aware of our spiritual needs. For some people, their awareness happens quietly, while for others it will happen during a life crisis.

When I Was Two Years Old

I'd like to share with you one of those times. It was when I was two years old; this was the first time my spiritual needs first became apparent to me.

It took place on a sunny summer day while I was visiting at my grandparent's apartment. We were visiting on that weekend, as we so often did. Everyone was busy chatting in the kitchen, but not grandpa. Grandpa was with me. He always wanted to be with me. You see, my grandfather and I had a very special relationship; I was his favorite, and his only grandchild.

Of course, at the young age of two, I was not really aware

of this fact, but what was very clear to me was that he loved me with a love that was far above everyone else's love toward me. I was his favorite, and somehow I knew it. He never got mad at me; he just loved me.

He made me smile, he made me giggle, and he made me happy, all the time. I just loved being with him. He was my favorite person in my whole little world. He talked a lot to me and I listened a lot. After all, a two-year-old's vocabulary is somewhat limited. But in my toddler way, I responded to what he said, and it was as if he always understood me. I found that amazing and just loved that about him. For certain, we were best buddies.

I remember the rays of sun streaming through the window and the fresh breeze blowing through the sheer curtains that hung in his bedroom. Grandpa was not feeling well at the moment, so he was resting in bed. That was ok. He told me to come sit by him anyway. So I hopped up next to him and cuddled up. We talked, we laughed, and things were as perfect as they always were.

I was so sure that my presence made him feel better. I was happy as could be, and so was he. Then, out of nowhere, something happened; something wasn't right. I watched the expression on my grandpa's face change. He looked as though he were in pain. Then he began to have difficulty breathing. I sat up straight and felt panic sweep through my body. I quickly tumbled off the bed and rushed out of the room into the kitchen to call everyone for help. Everyone ran into the bedroom. I did too. Everyone was shaken; there was rushing all around. I kept quiet. I stayed still. I stood right next to my grandpa's side. Slowly and gently, as I stood next to him, he leaned over and kissed me.

Then my dad stepped in and started pushing on my grandpa's chest. I was not sure why. Then I realized my dad was sharing the air from his mouth with my grandpa. I felt relieved. Grandpa just needed a bit more air.

But no, something still was not right. The atmosphere was now charged with a sense of urgency that was different than before. What my dad was doing wasn't working. My grandma quickly left the room to call the doctor. The doctor seemed to come right away, but not soon enough. When he walked in, he didn't say much, but he looked very sad as he left.

I knew that nothing was ok. I just stood there for what seemed like... forever. And there my grandpa lay. Not sleeping, just lifeless. I knew he was gone.

The next thing I remembered was several men, all dressed alike; they walked into the room and took my grandpa away.

I stood there. I watched them take him from me. I went to wave goodbye, but thought, what sense would that make, since my grandpa could not wave back to me anymore.

I sighed deeply and thought how I really didn't even get to say goodbye. The thought had never crossed my mind that my grandpa was going to be leaving me, not ever, and certainly not today. And then I was reminded of how he leaned over to kiss me. I realized this was his farewell-good-bye kiss to me... little did I know.

Without the ability to articulate, there was nothing I could say to anyone; I was not able to express my sorrow. Well, I guess it really didn't matter a whole lot since no one really knew how much I loved him anyway. They would not understand. Only I knew that, and only grandpa knew that. I slowly realized that I had been left to suffer my loss alone.

I stayed in his bedroom. Just walking around. Thinking. Feeling. Sensing how the room felt so quiet, like an empty place. Over and over I kept feeling how empty it was. Why was this feeling of emptiness resonating so much within me? Because that was the same way my heart was feeling, for within my heart I now felt... an empty space. No more laughing together, no more of his smiling at me, no more hugs from him. No more grandpa. In contrast, where the love of my grandfather used to be, there was just this empty space.

I Felt the Void

I felt it. It was a gap. A void. The love that had once filled my heart was now gone. I could only try to imagine the memories, but it was not the same. It was not as real. It was still so empty. And the emptiness hurt me; it made me cry. But then came a whisper from within my heart; a soft knowing that there was something more to this life than just the here and now.

But then came a whisper from within my heart; a soft knowing that there was something more to this life.

It was God who put that "knowing" there.

"God has put a sense of eternity in people's minds." (Eccl 3:11b GWT)

Out of this void came a knowing, a sureness of eternity.

Eternity was real.

Eternity was my hope.

Eternity was my future.

I just knew it. No one had to tell me. This brought hope into my despair and calmed my childlike spirit. Though I had lost my grandpa for now, some day I would have him back. He had gone somewhere to live forever, and someday forever I would go to meet him.

The Hope of Eternity

Although I was heartbroken beyond anything I had ever felt as a young child, the hope of eternity swept over me like a breath of fresh air. I was full of sorrow, but a soft breeze had swept over my heart carrying with it a song of hope.

Without anyone ever being able to tell me about "forever," I knew about the promise of eternity. I knew that this life was not the end, and that something greater was awaiting me. One day, grandpa and I would be together again, but this time, there would be no more goodbyes.

I don't remember much more about that day, but that night, when I was in my crib, I remember listening to my parents crying in their bed.

Little did they know, I was crying, too.

8

ETERNITY WITHIN EACH OF US

No one had to tell me. The soft whisper from within my heart let me know that there was something more to this life than what I could see with my eyes. I knew this. The reason I knew was because I had been designed with eternity in my heart.

"He has set eternity in the human heart…" (Eccl 3:11b) "He has made everything beautiful in its time. He has also set eternity in the human heart; yet no one can fathom what God has done from beginning to end." (Eccl 3:11) God is the creator of our hearts, and it is He who designed each one of us with "eternity in our hearts."

The God-Shaped Void

This God-given, God-placed, God-designed longing in our hearts is sometimes referred to as a "God-shaped void." This void tells us that there is something more to our lives than the temporary things we see around us.

It lets us know there is the hope of something more to this life; a need for something more in this life; and a promise and hope of something in and after this life that "has no end."

We may not be fully aware of it, but each person has an inner knowing that we have a need for something eternal in our lives. It is a sense that things in this temporary world cannot fully satisfy. This "eternity in our heart" creates in us that longing for something deeper.

The reality is that all the things in this world, including our mortal bodies, will eventually pass away. They all have an end. Yes, certainly there are so many good things in this world that God made for our pleasure and enjoyment; and yes, there is so much awe and wonder in the world around us that can bring us so much satisfaction; and yet, there is nothing in this temporal world that is "big" enough, "deep" enough, or "lasts long enough" to fill the "forever" in our hearts.
And this is the way we have all been designed... by God.

Trying to Fill the Void

People can spend a lifetime trying to fill that empty feeling. They look to things found in this world such as other people, possessions or power, but they are left unfulfilled. That is because the deepest longing of our hearts is found
Not in what we do,
What we attain,
What we own,
Or in how we look.

We will not find this deeper satisfaction in money, not in a spouse, not even in our kids, not in our family or in any person. Not even by becoming famous!
It is not found in recognition, accomplishments, or achievements.

There is nothing in this world that completely fills this void in our life.

The wisest, richest and most famous man of his time, who lived over three thousand years ago, lived a life then that might be referred to as a "lifestyle of the rich and famous" now. He was a king, and he possessed every conceivable thing that had the potential of bringing him satisfaction. He lacked nothing. He had it all. He was rich, and he was wise. His palace, known as Solomon's Temple, could have been considered one of the wonders of the world of its day. World leaders of that era would travel from afar to see it. They were awed and staggered by it.

Here is a quick glimpse of King Solomon's greatness:

- Each year Solomon received about twenty-five tons of gold. This did not include the additional revenue he received from merchants and traders, all the kings of Arabia, and the governors of the land. (1 Kings 10:14-15)
- People from every nation came to consult him and to hear the wisdom God had given him. The whole world wanted an audience with Solomon to hear the wisdom that God had put in his heart. (1 Kings 10:24)
- Solomon accumulated a huge force of chariots and horses. (1 Kings 10:26a)
- The king made silver as common in Jerusalem as stones. (1 Kings 10:27)

Solomon accumulated all of the best this world had to

offer, including riches, jewels, and possessions; he had the largest army and the greatest palace; he delved into profoundly intense studies, and even had hundreds of the most desirable woman available to him at his request. He pursued all of this and attained all of it.

He had "arrived."

And did all of this bring him to complete satisfaction?

No! Instead, do you know what he said?

He said he was grieved!

Hear his own words: "So I came to hate life, because what is done under the sun was grievous to me, for all is vanity, futile, and meaningless, like chasing and striving after the wind." (Ecc 2:17).

Solomon was not even happy. Not only was he grieved, but he had reached a point that he even hated life!

The Temporal Cannot Satisfy That Which Is Eternal

Solomon had discovered what so many of us spend a lifetime trying to learn: With every conceivable, imaginable, possible thing in this world that promises to fulfill us, it can never completely satisfy.

But why? Why don't the things of this world satisfy?

Because that which is *temporal* cannot satisfy that which is *eternal*.

Because that which is temporal cannot satisfy that which is eternal.

God purposefully designed us so that we could not find lasting satisfaction or enjoyment apart from His eternity. We can try, but in the end, we will still end up empty because that is the way God designed it, so we would have a need for Him.

Even if we have every earthly want, need, and dream fulfilled, if it is not of God, we will find ourselves feeling like something is missing.
Nothing in this temporary world can satisfy the eternal longing in our hearts.

Nothing in this temporary world can satisfy the eternal longing in our hearts.

How to describe this eternal longing?
This eternity in our hearts may be described as an awareness of something beyond ourselves.

This longing is one thing that sets us apart from the animal kingdom, for as humans we have this "mark of hunger." We hunger and thirst for something here on planet Earth that cannot satisfy. We have a thirst, a quest, and a pursuit for more. A need for eternity; ultimately, a need for God. Total contentment, deep peace, and complete satisfaction is not found in anything except God alone. Based on King Solomon's studies, as he searched for fulfillment in life, he noted many things that people look to in hopes of finding fulfillment.

Temporal Things Cannot Satisfy

Following is a list of things that Solomon considered. In the end, he concluded that these things were not enough to satisfy the longing of a person's heart. As we take a look at this list—a more contemporary version—let us ask ourselves, "Are we trusting in these things and hoping that they will bring us complete satisfaction?

- Wealth: More money, possessions, a new home, a new car, a new business, a better lifestyle, a new _____. (Fill in the blank with whatever you think will bring you happiness.)
- Fame: Honor, recognition, awards, talent, scholarships.
- People: Family, friends, marriage, a baby, kids, grandkids, pets.
- Work: A successful career, achievements, promotions.
- Hobbies: Sports, TV, movies, gaming, electronics, vacations.
- Health: Nutrition, the perfect diet, fitness, a great body, beauty.
- A good life: A long life, a simple life, a peaceful life.
- Education: Philosophy, deep-thinking, innovation, creativity.
- A Dream: A life-long quest, striving to fulfill a dream.

Many of these things are wonderful. And actually, they were made for our enjoyment. However, none of them are eternal; therefore, none of them can fully satisfy the eternity in our hearts. So, if these temporal things cannot satisfy us, then what is left?

Many people have asked this same question, and have not only come up with their own solutions, but have also come up with their own gods. The number of gods to choose from is countless and there are so many confusing messages today about which god or goddess is the "real one," and which one can really satisfy.

Although there are so many spiritual belief systems, religions, gurus, and theologies, to choose from, regardless of which religion, they all have one thing in common: Their gods are all *dead!*
All except one, who is Jesus Christ, who *rose from the dead.* Jesus said, "I am the Resurrection and the Life. The one who believes in Me will live, even though they die; and whoever lives by believing in Me will never die. Do you believe this?" (John 11:25-26)

I realize people may find this view as narrowminded or offensive, but what Jesus spoke often offended many: "And they were deeply offended and refused to believe in Him." (Matt. 13:57a)
Then Jesus told them, "A prophet is honored everywhere except in his own hometown and among his own family." (Matt. 13:57b)
Jesus came to Earth and made plain and clear who God is and who God is not; and His message and teachings are wrapped up in one book, called the New Testament.

In my hopes to clear up a few questions and misconceptions,

the following is a list of what I have learned about who God is and who He is not:

Who God Is Not

God is not an inanimate "higher power."
God is not "an object" or an "it."
He is not found in spiritism, yin-yang, or yoga.
He is not in Gnosticism or Buddhism.
He is not about "religion."
He is not found in new age or chi energy.
He is not in superstition or "old wives tales."
He is not some warm fuzzy feeling.
He is not a building.
He is not a cult.
He is not a she.
He is Father God, not mother nature.
He is not just a man.
He is not just a "good" man.
Nor is He just a good teacher.
He is not some sort of cosmic entity or energy.
He is not about human potential or Scientology.
He in not about holistic thinking.
He is not found in tha-chi, reike, or astrology.
He is not found in chakraz, crystals, or Krishna.
He is not found in Mohammad, or Buddha, or gurus.
He is not about reincarnation, channeling, or zen.
He has nothing to do with black magic, white magic, or witchcraft.
He has nothing to do with transcendental meditation.
He is not dead.

Today Jesus Himself asks you this question:
"But what about you?" He asked.
"Who do you say I am?" (Mark 8:29)
Jesus Christ is the visible image of the invisible God.

Jesus Christ is the visible image of the invisible God.

Who God Is

He is alive and speaking to you in a small, still voice.
He is telling you now who He is.
He is a person.
He is a father.

He is forgiving.

He is beyond capable, above competent, and He is in control.

He is omniscient.

He is omnipotent .

He is omnipresent.

He is unlimited.

He is everywhere at all times.

He is all seeing, all knowing, all loving.

He is a Triune God, Father, Son, and Holy Spirit; Three in One.

He sent His Son.

His Son, willingly, laid down His life.

His Son died and rose from the grave.

His Son is coming back again.

He lives. He speaks. He loves.

He cries. He laughs. He gets mad.

He gets disappointed. He can feel joy or pain.

This Father, who is a person, He is God.

He has many names:

His name is El-roi, "The God Who sees me."

His name is Immanuel, "God is with us."

And as Jesus so often referred to Him, His name is "Heavenly Father."

And this Father, who is in heaven, wants to be your dad.

He knows your name.

He knows when you were born.

He knows the number of hairs on your head.

He knows if you are sitting or standing,

He sees you when you're sleeping and

He knows when you're awake.

(And no, He is not Santa.)

He knows what you are going to say before you speak it.

Actually, He knows everything about you; even your future!

And why does He know all this about you?

Because that is how much He cares about you!

Only the True God who is "The way, the truth, and the life" (John 14:6) can satisfy the longing in our hearts.

You see, eternity in our hearts requires something eternal to satisfy it.

Based on this, we can conclude that our satisfaction for eternity can only be found in something that is itself eternal.

And something eternal cannot be found in some-*thing*, but only in Some-*one*.

Therefore, the eternity in our hearts can only be satisfied by The One Who Is Eternity;

The Only One Who is Eternal.

And the only who is all these things is the One Who is God.

He is The Eternal God. (Gen 21:33)

The One Who calls Himself, "I AM." (Ex 3:14b)

He is the only One

Who can satisfy the eternity we have in our hearts.

He is the only One Who can satisfy the eternity we have in our hearts.

Put God First

Yes, it is true that God can bring us satisfaction through many of these good these things found on King Solomon's list, but apart from God they cannot fully satisfy.

First we need to allow God to fill the eternity in our hearts. By first and foremost, filling the eternity in our hearts, then these other pleasures can be enjoyed with the proper perspective and meaning as we put God first in all we do. In His word He tells us: "In everything you do, put God first..." (Prov. 3:6a TLB)

9

BONDING, HURTS, AND LIES

When we put God first, the deepest longing of our hearts at last becomes satisfied. It is at this point that a deeper healing can begin.

So, let's start at the beginning.

As infants we are born *physically*, but in order for us fill the eternity in our hearts, we need to born *spiritually*.

It is this "new birth" that creates a healing bond between God and us.

It is this "new birth" that creates a healing bond between God and us.

This bonding is the most powerful part of being loved and accepted. When we bond with God, then true inner healing can really begin. First the healing will begin within ourselves, then the healing will overflow out onto our other relationships.

We are born spiritually when we receive Christ into our lives. Jesus called this experience the "new birth." Jesus explained to Nicodemus that "except a man be born again, he cannot see the Kingdom of God." (John 3:3) When we are born again, we become able to see and understand things about God that we could not before. Being born again is far more profound than we can understand, as it

is our being "born of the Spirit." (John 3:8)
Receiving Christ is the single most important decision a person can ever make in his or her life.

Receiving Christ is the single most important decision we will ever make in our life.

Not only does it fulfill our longings here on Earth, but we also receive the promise of eternal life. "For the wages of sin is death, but the gift of God is eternal life in Christ Jesus our Lord." (Romans 6:23)

Once we are "born anew," we become a new creature in Christ. This means that anyone who belongs to Christ has become a new person.
"The old life is gone; a new life has begun!" (2 Cor. 5:17)

A New Season

This new life is a wonderful season where God begins to help us pick up the broken pieces of our lives and put them back together, making us whole. As we begin to read His word and fellowship with others, we are refreshed and encouraged. As we go to God daily, reading His word, His "living water," (John 4:10) refreshes us. In our spirits we are "inwardly being renewed day by day." (2 Cor. 4:16)
Once Christ is the center of our lives we can begin to see things from a new perspective and He comes to "bind up our wounds." (Psalm 147:3b)

Healing From a Heavenly Perspective

Before we come to know God personally, we can receive help, good counsel, and restoration; however, when God is in the center of our lives and when He is involved in the healing process, so often the healing is more complete and much faster; and in some cases, even instantaneous! One example of this was a case in my own life where I needed emotional healing.

I was in extreme "emotional pain" and I could not figure out the cause of it. Then, while reading my Bible one day, a verse jumped off the page in answer to my exact question, and revealed the root of my problem. This accelerated the healing process and brought so much clarity. I still had to work through the hurts, but at least I knew the "diagnosis!"

When God is involved in the healing process, things can be revealed that might otherwise take a longer time to be discovered. The roots of things such as guilt, shame, condemnation, and rejection can be addressed from a heavenly perspective of our being unconditionally loved and fully forgiven by God Himself.

Once we have a personal relationship with God, we can experience a "peace that passes understanding." (Phil. 4:7) This does not necessarily mean that all our problems go away. But what is different is that He is there with us, working through each situation.
We are no longer alone.

Most of us have problems of some sort. Life can be hard.

During the course of our lives many things can come to wound us. Most of what we suffer from—whether it be losing a loved one, losing a home, losing our health, being betrayed, being forgotten or misunderstood—fits into one main category:

Loss.

In Life We Have Losses

Life is full of losses. We may lose a job, we lose a spouse, we lose a pet, we may lose an opportunity of a lifetime, we lose a child, or even lose our identity. These are all so painful. (Please know I am so sorry for the loss you have experienced.)

Even at every stage of life we feel a loss of some sort as we let go of that phase which is past.

Even at every stage of life we feel a loss of some sort as we let go of that phase which is past.

We suffer actual losses:

A toddler that has to begin let go of their pacifier and blankie,

A teen whose playtime is now replaced by chores and study time,

A young adult whose free time is replaced by work and family responsibilities,

An elderly person who loses many things such as health, financial stability, friends, and possibly the ability to care for themselves.

We can suffer abstract losses:
When people fail to acknowledge, understand or affirm our feelings, we suffer a loss of self-worth.
When our God-given longings are not met, so often these longings become the source of our pain.
These unfulfilled needs can damage us and cause long-term consequences.

What loss comes to your mind? What unmet needs? Everyone suffers loss of some sort, even as children.

Following is a story about a loss I suffered at age eleven. Afterwards, I would like to share a few "freeing principles" that I learned during the recovery process from this loss, as well as a variation of other freeing truths.

The Baby Story

I was eight years old, and this was a time when we welcomed foster children into our home. A child would stay at our house for a while until their family situation allowed for them to return to their home or be adopted by another family. Many times they were supposed to stay for a short while, but their stay was so often extended, and they would end up staying much longer.

After a particularly challenging teenager finished her stay with us, we got a call from the agency asking if we could take in a newborn baby, just for a couple of weeks. We were all very excited about this idea. We made all the needed preparations, crib and all.

She arrived. "Baby" is what I will call her. Baby was just seven days old. So tiny, fragile, and very sweet. The first few days I would observe her at arms length. I would get up early, and just watch her sleeping.

I would take mental notes as she was fed, changed, rocked, and put to bed, paying very close attention about how to care for a newborn.

I wanted to be with her all the time.

The first night of her stay, in the middle of the night, I heard her fussing. I jumped right out of bed to see if she was ok. I reached my hand into the crib and rubbed her back until she fell back asleep. This would become my new routine. A few days into our little midnight rendezvous, I realized if instead of rubbing her back, that if I nudged Baby, she would wake up, which was even better. Then if she started crying, that was really the best, since then she needed to be held. And since my mom did not want to be woken up, well, someone would have to comfort the newborn baby and stop her from crying. Oh well, I guess that someone would have to be me.

I was confident enough from my hours of informal trained supervision that I could pick Baby up out of the crib by myself. So, that is what I did. It was easy, and before I knew it, I was picking her up and placing her down with ease, just like a real mom would do.

Before sunrise I would get up and check on the baby. If in the early hours of the morning I noticed her diaper was wet, I knew enough about that to change her. And if she seemed a bit hungry, I knew how to heat up the bottle and give her some milk. And so began my playing house, except this time with a real baby. So before my mom ever woke up to check on the baby, she was already all taken care of… by me! I would then sneak back to bed as though nothing ever happened. It was our little secret; just between Baby and me.

The more I took care of the baby, the more time I wanted to spend with her. Baby and I, we had a special bond. I don't remember Baby ever crying when she was in my care. I had a sense that she knew me, trusted me and appreciated me.

During Baby's stay, I paid very close attention to any

phone calls that came in. I wanted to be there to hear the conversation about how long they would extend her stay. Sure enough, the call came, and they wanted us to keep her longer. This was the best news ever, and maybe they would even ask us to keep her permanently. I had my heart set on it! So the days continued, cuddling her and caring for her in the mornings, singing her to sleep at night. During the day my mom would take care of her, but I continued my secret morning and night shifts. If she fussed in the wee hours of the night, I would tiptoe out of my bed, making sure she was ok. Many times I picked her up, even though it really wasn't necessary, and put her back down after I had rocked her back to sleep in my arms. Each time I placed her gently back in her crib I would tell her how much I loved her, and could imagine her saying back to me, *Thank you for taking such good care of me. I love you, too.*

Days later another phone call came about the baby's stay. I was thrilled to no end, and felt so excited at the thought of being able to take care of this baby even longer, to watch her grow, and love her and give her all the attention she needed.

The foster agency called and asked if we were ready to give her back.
What? Give her back? That could not be possible. She would be staying longer, just as usual, like the other kids who stayed with us.

No, Baby was not. Baby was going back to her real mom.

But, but, but I felt like I… I was her real mom. I was the one who picked her up every time she cried. I was the one that was there for her. I fed her and I changed her. I was her mom (well, I knew I wasn't really her mom, but I felt like I was). The certainty of the situation hit me. She was only with us for a while, and like the other foster children, Baby would have to leave us.

This was going to be too hard to handle. How could I let her go? No. I just can't go through this. The thought of someone taking one of my toy doll babies away from me was too traumatizing, how could I even begin to think of the pain that I was going to feel if someone took my real Baby away from me?
Reality began to strike. Someday soon a foster agent would come to take my baby away.

Before I knew it, the day had arrived. Holding back the tears, I helped pack her belongings. I made sure she had all of little baby things, booties, blankets, diapers and all. I knew what was hers better than anyone else.

Her baby bag was packed and our relatives also came that day to say farewell. I remember everyone standing in our living room, each one taking their turn, kissing Baby good-bye. I felt so sad as I watched. I felt so weak that I had to sit. I sat down on the wooden bench with my back against the wall, and that was exactly how I felt, backed against a wall; completely trapped. I sat there looking out at all that was happening; it was so hard to accept. It felt as though it was not real. But I knew it was.

Then the foster agent lady came and took her. I wanted to blame the foster agent, but I knew it was not her fault. There was a lot of commotion, everyone saying goodbye and all. And then, it was over. My family went into the kitchen to have cake and coffee without anyone saying a word to me.

What? Was I the only one in pain? No one seemed that devastated, just me. No one even acknowledged me or came to talk to me to ask how I was feeling or what I was thinking. They had no idea what I was experiencing! I was there feeling the loss of a child, my own child, and my parents and family went off into the kitchen to chat?

I was confused, I was hurt and I was mad! But maybe worst of all, lost in my grief, I felt so alone. I didn't know what to do. I so desperately needed to talk to someone and to be comforted.
I felt like running away.

I contemplated sharing my feelings with someone in the family; but I thought, "What difference would it make to try to share how I felt with them when they would never understand what I was feeling anyway? How could they?" After all, no one was nearly as attached to Baby as I was. I was the one who had spent so much time with her, holding her feeding her and loving her. I was closest to her.

I knew they could not understand. They had not understood me in any of my past situations either, so why would this one be any different?

Everyone finally left, and it was time for bed. As I expected, neither my mom nor my dad came to ask how I was doing. I was really hurt, but not so much by what they did, but rather, by what they did not do. I was wounded by neglect. Such was the usual pattern in my life as I, again, was left to suffer in alone and in silence.

Looking back, I can understand better what was happening during this event. But at the time, I only felt hurt, rejection, and despair.

Here are the Twelve Freeing Truths I learned:

Twelve Freeing Truths
1. Unspoken rules

I realized that the main reason I was not free to share my feelings with my family was due to their "unspoken rules." There was a silent understanding that you:

- Don't talk,
- Don't feel, and
- Don't trust.

The result of living with these unspoken rules ends in what are called "frozen emotions." In this environment no one is safe to share their feelings. Particularly for children, the consequence of living with these rules is a "self" shrouded by shame.

Shame is much worse than guilt, because you can ease the pain of guilt by apologizing, whereas shame becomes ingrained, causing a person to feel of no or little value, and to feel worthless.

Shame is much worse than guilt.

---

2. Real or imagined losses

I learned that when you lose something, the loss can be real or imagined; either way the hurt is the same. In this case, I did not really lose my own baby, and yet I felt and experienced the loss of my own child. I had felt as though I was her mom, when in fact, I was not. Yet, my hurt was just as deep.

When we suffer a loss, whether it's real or imagined, the loss is equally significant.

When we suffer a loss, whether it's real or imagined, the loss is equally significant.

For both types of losses, we need to work through the same grieving process.

3. Lack of intention

People—in this case my family and parents—can be totally unaware of how they are hurting others. It is so important to know, however, that just because someone hurts us unintentionally does not change the impact of the offense. Our hurt is still just as real. For example, if I were to unintentionally bump into someone and they fell and got hurt, my being unintentional would not make their injury hurt any less!

It's not unusual that when people hurt us unintentionally, they will deny their thoughtless actions. They may make statements such as, "Well, what I did wasn't that bad." That is denial on their part, and this does not lessen the damage or hurt that we may experience. Also, if the abuse is by neglect, this pain is also just as significant and real.

There are many ways people deny or excuse their hurting others. Here is a list of the general forms of denial. If you're trying to work through a situation with others where there is denial, this list can come in handy as a great sanity check for you!

- Forgetting
- Outright denial
- Blaming
- Indirect admission
- Mystical excuses
- Minimizing
- Avoidance
- Grasping for straws
- Easy way out

If we feel pain, there is a reason.

4. Denial can result in two different realities
When people are unaware that they hurt us, it can be

because they are in denial. If you are unsure if they are in denial, you may chose to gently confront them. However, be ready to accept that they may or may not be able to acknowledge the wrong they have done.

If a person is in denial, it's very common that they will respond with anger.

When there is denial, it as though there are two different realities.

As was in my case, *their* reality was that they had done no wrong, but *my* reality was that they had harmed me. When others cannot see our side of the story, we may have to accept that we may be permanently misunderstood.

We are told to "Come, let us reason together," (Isaiah 1:18) but people who are in denial have nothing to reason with, because in their mind, the problem you are talking about does not exist!

Denial is not rational, so it is not open to reasoning!

Denial is not rational so it is not open to reasoning!

---

5. Blaming

It is very sad when people do wrong and then don't take responsibility for their own actions. Instead of admitting their sin against us, they blame us instead. We need to respond to this, but how?

We can see what the correct way of responding by looking at how God responded to people who blamed. The first blame game took place in the Garden of Eden. Did you notice there was one thing that Adam and Eve never did after they sinned? They never said they were sorry. (I sometimes wonder what may have been different if they had.) God gave them an opportunity to admit their wrong by going to them and asking, but He never forced them to apologize, and they chose not to.

These are the six things we can learn: When someone sins by doing wrong against us, we are to:

1. Go to them

Go to them and ask, "Have you done this?" We are not to accuse them, but to give them an opportunity to be aware of their wrong and admit their error.

In the Garden of Eden, this was the conversation:

God asked, "Who told you that you were naked? Have you eaten from the tree that I commanded you not to eat from?"

The man said, "The woman you put here with me— she gave me some fruit from the tree, and I ate it."

Then the Lord God said to the woman, "What is this you have done?"

The woman said, "The serpent deceived me, and I ate." (Gen 3:11-13)

Adam blamed God by saying, "The woman whom

You gave to be with me, she gave me from the tree, and I ate." (Gen. 3:12)

Then Eve blamed the serpent by saying, "The serpent deceived me." (Gen 3:13)

Adam and Eve did not take responsibility for the wrong they had done and notice,

God never forced them to. God was sad, hurt and deeply disappointed, but He did not insist that they confess their sin to Him.

2. Do not to force an apology

We are not to force the person for an apology or to admit the wrong they have done. We should be prepared for the person to deny their wrong, which will cause us to feel sad, hurt and disappointed, too. (We will be pleasantly surprised and thrilled if they are humble and apologize!)

One consequence of their sin was that both Adam and Eve were punished and would have pain; Eve would have "very severe pain in childbearing," and Adam would have "painful toil" working the land in order to eat.

3. Feel pity, not guilty

There will be painful consequences for the person who

sins and blames and does not repent. And we are to feel pity for them, but not feel guilty that we caused their pain, for we did not; rather, it was their own sin and their wrong choice that caused the predicament. Sadly, they are reaping what they sowed.

God banished Adam and Eve from the garden. He no longer would walk in the garden with them each day.

4. Limit communiction

Based on this response, we can feel it is sensible to limit distance and communication with a person who blames us. (The extent to which you are able to do this will depend on your circumstance.) We should try to keep our distance in whatever way that is possible and appropriate, without our stepping over a line into sin. If we cannot distance ourselves physically, then we can focus on guarding our heart, mind, and emotions.

5. Expect to go through a grieving process.

As we respond by distancing ourselves in order to protect ourselves, we should keep in mind that the other person, or persons, who are guilty of "blaming" will suffer consequences and be in pain, similar to how Adam and Eve's punishment involved pain. It is important that we realize that their pain is not our fault; rather it is a result of their own wrongdoing for not being willing to repent and admit their sin. Out of compassion, we will also suffer pain from seeing them hurt. We will also experience disappointment, being let down, and possibly even feeling betrayed. We will suffer the loss of the relationship, as well as the bond of a relationship we had thought we had, or hoped to have. Either way, a grieving process will result.

6. Be angry, but do not sin.

When Adam and Eve chose to blame, God banished them and cast them out. God was hurt, but God was angry, as well. The word "banish" expresses a driving out, an expelling, forcing someone away as punishment, to throw out. So we can expect to feel angry, too. (This is a good time for us to practice our being angry without sinning.)

6. Don't belittle suffering

No hurt is insignificant. When we compare our problems or hurts with others, and are thankful our situation was not or is not as severe as someone else's, we often minimize our own trauma. This is not fair to ourselves. Yes, we are correct to be thankful, but we are not correct to minimize or belittle our suffering. "God does not belittle the suffering of the needy." (Psalm 22:24a)

For example, if a child falls and scrapes her knee, it would not be considerate to tell her to stop complaining because another child had a more severe injury. This approach would not be acknowledging or validating the child's pain. It also would not be sensitive or nurturing.

Each person's hurt, whether big or small, is to be

acknowledged. No hurt is insignificant. Certainly the injury is to be brought into perspective, but no pain is to be despised. "For He has not ignored or belittled the suffering of the needy. He has not turned his back on them, but has listened to their cries for help." (Psalm 22:24)

Since God does not belittle any person's pain, neither should we. Not only are we not to despise someone else's pain, but we are not to despise our own. "A broken and a contrite heart, O God, You will not despise." (Ps. 51:17) God has pity on you. God is merciful to you. He is rich in mercy toward you. "God, Who is rich in mercy, because of his great love for us." (Eph. 2:4a)

And so, we are to love ourselves and love others the way

God loves us. Remember, God does not belittle our suffering, so neither should we.

What a wonderful thought that such a great God does not
despise even our smallest hurts.

**What a wonderful thought that such a Great God does
not despise even our smallest hurts.**

One of my favorite illustrations of how God does not
despise even our smallest hurt was taught by Jesus, when
He talked about the sparrows. "What is the price of two
sparrows—one copper coin? But not a single sparrow can
fall to the ground without your Father knowing it." (Matt
10:29)

A sparrow is not worth much, yet the Father takes notice.
If God cares so much for a sparrow that is so insignificant,
we can only begin to understand how much compassion
He feels towards us. Even the smallest injury to the insignificant and unnoticed bird touches the heart of the caring
Father; so how much more must even our smallest hurt
move Him with compassion for us? After all, so far as
value, our worth cannot be compared to the sparrow. One
sparrow cost only half a copper coin, whereas our cost was
the immeasurable price of the life of God's own Son; the
Son who willingly laid down Himself to offer us His gift
of eternal life.

In light of this, our value, when compared to the sparrow's value, is infinite.

So, if God cares so much for one sparrow whose worth cannot compare to ours, then how much does He care about our suffering? Yes, more than we can comprehend. And to emphasize His point, Jesus adds, "So don't be afraid; you are worth more than many sparrows." (Matt. 10:31)

We are not insignificant to God and He includes this fact that "even the very hairs of your head are all numbered." (Matt. 10:30) right in between these two verses about the sparrows! This story is not "for the birds," it is for us, and all about His knowing us, being compassionate towards us, and our significance to Him!

7. Forgive, for they know not

I learned that I had no right to hold the offender as "guilty." There are several reasons to choose to forgive.

- One is the fact that I am not perfect either. "We all fall short of the glory of God." (Romans 3:23) Another reason is that two thousand years ago Christ died for me, long before I said I was sorry for my sins and faults. God did not wait for me to repent; He forgave me even before I knew I needed forgiveness, and even before I was born. While we were yet sinners, Christ died for us. And we are to forgive one another "just as in Christ God forgave you." (Eph. 4:32) So too, we are to forgive before our perpetrator asks for forgiveness. Even if they never do.

- We are to follow God's example of how to love. And as Christ hung on the cross and said, "Father, forgive them for they know not what they do," (Luke 23:34) on that day the rulers and the crowd, on one hand, knew what they were doing so far as demanding that Jesus be crucified; but on the other hand, they did *not* understand what they were doing, "for if they understood it they would not have crucified the Lord of glory." (1 Cor. 2:8) Many times people are not fully aware of what they are doing wrong and the consequences they are causing. So we too must forgive them, for they know not what they do. It is not our responsibility to pay them back for their wrong done against us. That is up to God. "Do not take revenge, my dear friends, but leave room for God's wrath, for it is written: 'It is mine to avenge; I will repay,' says the Lord." (Rom 12:19) Choosing not to forgive is like poisoning ourselves.

- If we decide not to forgive, we hold on to a small seed of anger that can cause resentment to grow, and over time it can turn into a root of bitterness. We are warned to "watch out (make sure, see to it) that no poisonous root of bitterness grows up to cause trouble (to destroy) and defile many." (Heb. 12:15) Unforgiveness is poison that grows and will cause trouble in your life and will cause damage to many people around you.

Unforgiveness is poison that grows and will cause trouble in your life and will cause damage to many people around you.

- Please keep in mind, when we choose to forgive, it may take a while for our feelings to catch up. That's ok, because feelings take time to heal too!

- The litmus test of whether or not we have completely forgiven someone is when we have come to terms with their not owing us anything. *Nothing.* That includes trying to reason with them or having them understand us.

We need to:

1. Let go of needing an apology from them.
2. Choose to stop trying to explain our point of view to them.
3. Stop expecting them to understand us.
4. Accept that they still think that we are wrong and they are right.

We even have to let go of the offender "agreeing to disagree." Full forgiveness is when you are content with being misunderstood and you are ok with the fact that the other person will stay convinced that they were right and you were wrong.

8. Abandonment

When I felt overlooked and insignificant, it caused me to feel abandoned.

When we are emotionally abandoned it leaves a "hole in our soul."

Over time, abandonment results in many problems related to compulsivity.

A part of abandonment is rejection, which can cause a great deal of insecurity, negativity, and deep feelings of worthlessness your life.

A part of abandonment is rejection, which can cause a great deal of insecurity, negativity, and deep feelings of worthlessness in our life.

These deep hurts can cause us deep heartache, beyond our ability to express. At times we can even find ourselves unable to be comforted, even As we cry out to God for help:

"I cried out to God for help; I cried out to God to hear me." (Ps. 77:1)

"When I was in distress, I sought the Lord; at night I stretched out untiring hands, my soul refused to be comforted." (Ps. 77:2)

To help us recover from this anguish, we can we can talk to ourselves and say:

Why, my soul, are you downcast?

Why so disturbed within me?

"Put your hope in God, for I will yet praise Him, my Savior and my God." (Ps. 43:5)

9. Look beyond the person

Something that is going on behind the scenes needs to be brought to our attention. In the same way God is *for* us, there is an enemy who is *against* us. There is a God good who is good, and an enemy who is evil. "The thief comes only to steal and kill and destroy. I came that they may have life and have it abundantly." (John 10:10)

God is real and the enemy is real. Satan is the author of the harm that comes our way, and people are just the tool that Satan uses to get to us. The person's intent may very well have been to do us harm, but God turns it around, and in due time, uses it for our good and for His purpose. As Joseph said to his brothers who intentionally betrayed him, threw him in a pit, then sold him into slavery: "You intended to harm me, but God intended it for good to accomplish what is now being done, the saving of many lives." (Gen 50:20)

Satan is the author of fear and the father of lies. "He is a liar and the father of lies." (John 8:44c) Satan's goal is to kill us, steal from us, and destroy us. That is why we are warned to "Be alert and of sober mind. Your enemy the devil prowls around like a roaring lion looking for someone to devour." (1 Peter 5:8) But we do not need to dwell on Satan, for he is defeated; but we need to be mindful of his tactics to devour us!

10. Family is not everything

This may sound a bit offensive to some people, but we need to be careful to keep our family in proper perspective. Even our mother and father are not to define us. Jesus made this point when his family was outside waiting for him. "While Jesus was still talking to the crowd, his mother and brothers stood outside, wanting to speak to him. Someone told him, "Your mother and brothers are standing outside, wanting to speak to You." He replied to him, "Who is my mother, and who are my brothers?" And stretching out His hand toward His disciples, He said, "Here are my mother and my brothers! For whoever does the will of my Father in heaven is my brother and sister and mother." (Matthew 12:46-50)

And why was it that his mother and brothers "stood outside?" Why was everyone else so interested to hear what Jesus had to say, but they were not? Because sometimes our physical family, those who are the closest to us, may not value us as they ought. Even Jesus said, "But I tell you the truth, no prophet is accepted in his own hometown." (Luke 4:24)

Jesus was not being esteemed or appreciated by his own family. But He pointed to those were closest to Him, His disciples who were fully supportive of Him. They were His closest friends who were "doing the will of the Father." We are to "Honor our father and our mother" (Ex. 20:12a) and as children we are to obey our parents. "Children, obey your parents in the Lord, for this is right." (Eph 6:1)

Notice that we are told to honor our parents "in the Lord." This point is very important because if our parents do not do or say what is in agreement with what the Lord teaches us, or if what they say or how they treat us does not line up with the word of God or how He treats us, then we are not to receive it.
This does not give us the right to be disrespectful toward our parents or family, but we must be sure that God's principles and views are what we obey and receive.

What God says and thinks about us must count the most;

neither our parents nor our family are to dictate to us who we are.

What God says and thinks about us must count the most.

How Our Heavenly Father feels about us, and His opinion of us, are to be the most significance influences in our lives. Our priority is to please God, obey Him, and have His approval. We are not to allow people's wrong opinions, or what people may say, think, or feel about us, to dominate us or defeat us. What God says and thinks about us must always remain paramount in our minds and hearts.

11. Rejection

I was rejected to the point I felt I had no value. Rejection had caused me to swallow the lie of guilt and shame. I was tricked into believing that the neglect and other hurts I had experienced were not only my imagination, but they were all my fault. Guilt made me feel that what I had *done* was bad, but even worse, the shame made me feel that I *was* bad.

Whether we've been rejected by what someone said or by what they did, either way it leaves us feeling less valued, and in more extreme cases, even worthless. We may think it didn't affect us much, but since our self-concept comes largely from our perceptions of others' opinions and from our perceptions others' love for us, a rejection can affect us. The truth is that rejection always hurts us. It is very important for us not to minimize any rejection we have experienced.

The fact is that rejection is the root of many emotional problems.

The fact is that rejection is the root of almost ALL emotional problems.

So, if you have been rejected at any time in your life, please take a moment to reflect ... is it possible you have hurts you were not aware of?
Here are a few suggestions to help you as you reflect on the times you may have felt rejected:

- Don't "make light" of the time you felt rejected.
- Accept the wrongs done against you.
- Allow yourself to feel the pain.
- Begin resolving any anger without being overly critical of yourself.
- Grieve the loss, real or imagined.
- Be responsible for how you responded.
- Forgive by releasing any resentment or bitterness.
- Realize your true identity; while others may reject you, God never does.

Awareness is key. Once we are able to and accept our hurts, and recognize our own self-destructive patterns, then we can begin to take steps toward healing.

All things work together. Healing is lifelong process, and God promises to work all things together, even our hurts, for our good.

"And we know that in all things God works for the good of those who love him, who have been called according to his purpose." (Romans 8:28)

Since God works all things together, that means that nothing in our lives is wasted, not even our pain.

"And after you have suffered a little while, the God of all grace, who has called you to his eternal glory in Christ, will Himself restore, confirm, strengthen, and establish you." (1 Peter 5:10) In the end, we will be restored.

"Let perseverance finish its work so that you may be mature and complete, not lacking anything." (James 1:4) In the end, we will be mature and complete.

"But He knows the way that I take; when he has tested me, I will come forth as gold." (Job 23:10)

We are being refined similar to how gold is refined by fire. So do not despair, in the end, our fiery trials will end up being the very things that make us shine!

12. Trust

There are certain characteristics of a person we can trust. Trust is not something to be given freely; rather, trust is something that is earned. Even if the person is a parent or relative, they too need to show they are worthy of our trust. It is natural that we assume that our parents and family are trustworthy, but unfortunately, those who are closest to us often feel more relaxed and thus can have a sense of entitlement. Too often, this is how abuse happens.

So how do we determine if a person is trustworthy?

For a person to earn our trust they need to have certain qualities. We can't just go by what we feel. If the person lacks these trustworthy qualities, we are to be wise and guard our heart. Regardless if they are family or not, if they are not trustworthy, we are not obligated to trust them. Family members are not exempt just because they are family; that does not entitle them to treat someone improperly, disrespectfully, or abusively. A person, including a family member or close friend, has to show they are trustworthy before we chose to trust them.

So what qualities are we to look for to know if someone merits our trust?
We can find the components of trust by asking a basic question:
"Can we trust what they "S.A.I.D.?"
Trust consists of these four main components:

> **Sincerity.** They are genuine in what they said and what they do. They have our best interest at heart. They are empathetic and understanding, not critical and condemning. They communicate openly and honestly. "Being quick to listen and slow to speak." (James 1:19b)

> **Ability.** They are capable of doing what they say. They have the skills to deliver what they commit to. They

must be competent.

Integrity. They are honest about what they say and do. They are worthy of your respect. They have high moral standings to do what is right, no matter what the cost. They must be compassionate and considerate and possess the fruits of the spirit: love, joy, peace, patience, kindness, gentleness, self-control.

Durability. They stick to what they said; they keep their word. They maintain and uphold what they agree to over a length of time. They are consistent. The keep their promises. They are reliable!

4 Components of Trust

TRUST

Belief in, reliance upon, and confidence in the Sincerity, Ability, Integrity and Durability of one other.

Sincerity	Ability	Integrity	Durability
transparency	capable	honesty	stable
openness	competent	truthful	sturdy
earnest devotion	skillful	fairness	resilient
no hypocrisy	knowledgeable	authenticity	permanence
real and personal	experienced	credibility	good track record
genuine	able to perform	good morals	reliability over time
caring		uprightness	consistency
pure intentions		good reputation	
good communicator		selflessness	
wholehearted			
understanding			
pure motives			
humility			

This chart above is a more complete list of the four components of trust.

Note: Please keep in mind these components indicate a person is trustworthy, not perfect; and that is ok because neither are we!

If these four components are visible, then is safe to open your heart, and with reasonable expectations, have a close and fulfilling relationship, filled with trust.

Keep in mind, people are imperfect, and will have varying degrees in all four of these areas. For example; a person may be lacking in one or more of these components of trust. They may be sincere and have integrity, but lack ability and durability. In these cases, you can trust, but only to a certain degree. It is likely that a person will feel offended that you don't trust them completely. Especially if they have low self-esteem, they may feel you are criticizing and judging them. In spite of this, you are not obligated to trust them in the areas they are not yet fully trustworthy. As gently, and lovingly as possible, you can explain this to them if necessary and only if you feel they are open to understand.

Without trust it is impossible to have a successful relationship. An atmosphere of trust is created as we humbly prefer the other person. Without trust, people cannot work together in a peaceful way.

Trust grows when we have humility toward one another. We are encouraged to "do nothing from selfishness or empty conceit, but with humility of mind regard one another as more important than yourselves." (Phil. 2:3) Trust in a relationship generates confidence in each person and causes the relationship to become mature and secure. Trust is a key component of the love we share. "Love always protects, always trusts, always hopes, always perseveres." (1 Cor 13:7)

10

GOOD GUILT AND BAD GUILT

We can spend a lifetime feeling guilty and not even be sure of the reason why.

You may have just a small bit of guilt, but it's enough that you find it irritating. Sometimes, in more extreme cases, there is an engraved mindset of guilt where the person feels guilty for just about everything they do… or don't do. Nothing they do ever seems to be right or good enough. They are wrong if they "do," and wrong if they "don't."

The good news is that not all guilt is bad. There is "good guilt" and "bad guilt." Good guilt is *constructive*. It softens us to *better* our lives.

Bad guilt is *destructive*. It crushes us and tries to *steal* our lives.

Sometimes it's easy to confuse the two types of guilt because, originally neither one of them makes us feel good about ourselves. The good guilt comes from *conviction*. The bad guilt comes from *condemnation*.

Conviction

Conviction is good because it corrects us and allows us hope to fix our wrong.

It is our conscience and our moral compass of right and wrong that guides us.

If a person refuses to listen to their conscience over and

over, their conscience has become deadened, or what is called seared. "These people are hypocrites and liars." (1 Tim. 4:2) But for those whose conscience is pure, and who are sincere, conviction is a positive force that makes them feel good guilt.

Good guilt is a healthy emotion that prompts us to abandon a wrong behavior, to seek forgiveness, and then to change and do what is right.

Conviction is good in that we can do something to fix it. At first we feel bad, but when then we admit our error, with sincere sorrow, with what is called "godly sorrow," (1 Cor. 7:11a) asking forgiveness from both God and the person, we can be forgiven; and as we move forward, we can be healed. "Therefore confess your sins to each other and pray for each other so that you may be healed." (James 5:16) As result of our true repentance, our guilt is grieved and then relieved. In the end we are healed and it brings us life.

Condemnation

Bad guilt comes from condemnation.

Condemnation is bad because it accuses us and leaves us helpless. In the end, it does not heal us; rather, it brings us death. This is not to be taken lightly, as condemnation can do a serious amount of damage in our lives.

Even as Christians, we can live a life filled with needlessly condemning ourselves. Condemnation is not like guilt. Guilt we can confess and correct; condemnation we cannot. With condemnation, even if we admit we are wrong, it does not help. Saying we are sorry and repenting does not fix our situation because condemnation is not about *the wrong we have done*, it is far worse; it is about *who we are*. Condemnation makes us feel that we, in the core of our being, are bad. A person who suffers from condemnation will be familiar with the feelings listed here:

- Feeling they're not good enough.
- Finding it hard to receive a compliment.
- Often putting themselves down.
- Telling themselves they just can't do things right.
- Feeling hard to love or feeing unlovable.
- Picking on themselves for every small thing.
- Frequently saying they would've, could've, should've.
- Wondering why what they do is never good enough.

If you or someone you know is struggling with condemnation, it is helpful to understand more about it, so you can understand how to help overcome it.

The Feelings of Condemnation

The first person who felt condemnation was Adam, in the garden. Adam's one sin brought condemnation on himself and on everyone. "Yes, Adam's one sin brings condemnation for everyone." (Rom. 5:18a)

To better understand the feelings of condemnation, let's look at what Adam and Eve experienced when they disobeyed and were sentenced to die; when they were condemned.

"But you must not eat from the tree of the knowledge of good and evil, for when you eat from it you will certainly die." (Gen. 2:17)

"When Adam and Eve sinned, they realized they were naked." (Gen 3:7)

They first thing Adam and Eve felt as a result of condemnation was their nakedness. The Greek root word for naked means "helpless." So, their first feelings of condemnation were:

- Being naked, and
- Helpless.

What happened next?

Their being naked caused them to hide. "And they were afraid because they were naked; so they hid." (Gen 3:10)

They felt:

- Afraid, and
- Forced into hiding.

The definition of hide is to keep out of sight, to conceal from the view or notice of others. They hid because they felt condemned. Now they also felt:

- Self-conscious and embarrassed,
- Uncomfortable,
- Uneasy and nervous.

Shame Is a Painful Feeling

Before Adam and Eve sinned, they felt no shame. "Adam and his wife were both naked, and they felt no shame; they were not ashamed." (Gen 2:25) But after they sinned, that all changed, and now they felt

- Shame
- And, in turn, were ashamed of themselves.

The Greek root word for "ashamed" has many bad implications.

Here are a few:

- To be astonished.
- To be confounded.
- Put to silence.
- To blush in the sense of paleness and terror.
- To be overwhelmed with unexpected calamity.
- To be troubled, disturbed, and confused in the mind.

Shame is a painful feeling of humiliation or distress, guilt, or embarrassment. Shame makes us feel guilty. Shame makes us feel defective, and that something is wrong with us. Shame can make us feel so extremely guilty that we can reach a point where we believe the lie that everything is our fault! I know, because I did! Shame carries with it a feeling of regret because you feel you have done something wrong; you feel embarrassed or self-conscious. Shame robs our peace and makes us feel as though we always fall short.

While you may not experience all of these feelings mentioned here, just struggling with one or a few of these emotions is enough to cause a problem. Whether it's one major hurtful incident or many smaller hurtful instances occurring over and over in your life, both are enough to seriously damage you and cause you deep inner pain.

Not only does a person struggling with condemnation feel this shame, but the person so often feels they *are* these things. They actually *become* these things.

For example:
A person does not just feel helpless; they believe they are helpless.

They don't just feel embarrassed about what they did; they are embarrassed about who they are.

They don't feel they caused a problem; they believe they are the problem.

A person who feels condemnation does not just feel they "did" something wrong, they feel they "are" wrong.

A person who feels condemnation does not just feel they "did" something wrong, they feel they "are" wrong.

They believe there is something wrong with them. Condemnation makes a person feel, that no matter what they do, it is never enough and it is never right; that they are never enough or right. This condemnation becomes ingrained in them and becomes a part of them.

They don't just feel as though they did something bad; they feel that they *are* bad.

The Solution

Now that we have a bigger picture of what these awful feelings of condemnation are, let us go look at the solution that we might be freed from these horrible feelings! Let us look at how Adam and Eve approached the solution.

In order to fix their feelings of being ashamed and condemned, Adam and Eve attempted to cover themselves. "And they suddenly felt shame at their nakedness. So they sewed fig leaves together to cover themselves." (Gen.3:7b)

They tried to cover their nakedness and shame by themselves. Did that work? No. That was not good enough because we see that "the Lord God came and made for Adam and for his wife garments of skins and clothed them." (Gen 3:21)

Adam and Eve's own solution did not suffice. God had to come and provide a better way. By this example, we can conclude that we are unable to fix our problem of condemnation on our own. If Adam and Eve needed God to come and help fix their condemnation problem, then so do we. We can find God's solution for us in the Bible. He tells us, "For there is now no condemnation for those who are in Christ Jesus. (Rom. 8:1)
Our solution to being freed from the feelings of condemnation is found where?
In Christ Jesus.
Because, in Christ, we find forgiveness for our sins.
It is in Him we are no longer condemned.

It is by substitution and divine grace we no longer have condemnation—not because of ourselves, or what we have done; and not by our trying to put on fig leaves, or something else, to try to cover our shame.

It is the great exchange. Our sin for His righteousness.

We are freed from condemnation only by God's coming to us. We are released from our being condemned as He exchanges our filthy rags, and our torn fig leaves, by He,

Himself, placing on us clothes of righteousness.
It is the great exchange. Our sin for His righteousness.

No, we don't deserve it. But that is why it is called grace.
Grace is something we cannot earn, it is not deserved.
"Grace is the gift of God." (Eph. 2:8b)
"God made Him who had no sin to be sin for us, so that
in Him we might become the righteousness of God." (2
Cor. 5:21)
Jesus Christ does not condemn us, He came to save us. "For
God did not send his Son into the world to condemn the
world, but to save the world through Him." (John 3:17)
So, in answer to our question, our freedom from condemn-
nation is found… in Christ.

The Accuser

So if God is not condemning us, then who is? It is possible
that we are condemning ourselves. But on a deeper level,
it is the enemy who is accusing us.
The author of all condemnation is Satan.
Satan is called "The Accuser." The root of the problem is
the enemy who condemns us. He is called the "Accuser
of the brethren."

**It is not God who condemns us, the enemy does. So
when we condemn ourselves, we are allowing the
enemy to destroy us.**

"For the one who accuses our brothers, who accuses them

day and night in the presence of our God, has been cast out." (Rev 12:10b)

It is not God who condemns us, the Enemy does. So when we condemn ourselves, we are allowing the enemy to destroy us.

The Devil is the one who comes to kill, steal, and destroy. Satan is the one who wants us to have bad guilt and feel condemned.

Satan says to us, "Yes, there is condemnation for you." But God says to us, "No, there is not."
Who will we chose to believe is right?

Satan is the thief. The thief comes only to steal and kill and destroy; but God never comes to deprive us, take from us, or rob from us. Jesus came that "we may have life, and have it to the full." (John 10:10)
For those people who struggle with condemnation, you may feel guilty by just reading this; you even may feel guilty about your "not supposed to be feeling guilty"!

If you are in Christ and still have condemnation, realize that God is not the one condemning you; it can be that it is you who are condemning yourself.
Please don't feel guilty about this. I am saying this because I did this to myself for years. I fell for the lies of accusing myself. I felt accused, and didn't even know it. I just felt "bad," and guilty, I had no idea I was accusing myself; that I was allowing the enemy to accuse me. I had become my

own worse enemy!

I had no idea I was accusing myself; that I was allowing the enemy to accuse me. I had become my own worse enemy!

Please don't despair. It takes a while for people to get into condemnation; it usually takes a while to get out of it. Just keep in mind that the solution will require the person's participation and their willingness to change the way they see themselves.
Please keep in mind that condemnation is a severe injury to our "self," and it takes time to heal.

Condemnation is a severe injury to our "self," and it takes time to heal.

An Illustration: The Rocks

Anyone can get stuck in condemnation, even people who believe in Christ. Through this illustration, I will explain how we can get stuck in it and how we can get out of it. The story takes place in the first century but is just as relevant to us today.

There was a woman who had done wrong and everybody knew about it. That in itself was already terribly degrading for the woman, but in addition to the guilt of her mistake, some arrogant people decided to expose her and make an example out of her.

The accusers brought the woman to be judged and to
be condemned.
The crowd was about to sentence the woman, whose crime,
according to the laws of that day, was punishable by death.
She was about to get the punishment she rightly deserved.
She was condemned to die. The accusers were all standing
up in front of her, ready to stone her to death; each one
held a stone in their hand.

We need to stop here for a minute and I need to ask you
to play a role in this story, and identify with the woman
who is standing in front of the crowd. There she stands,
alone and ashamed, feeling completely worthless and like
a complete failure. (If you are struggling with guilt and
condemnation, you are familiar with these feelings.)
She is guilty of the crime. The particular sin is irrelevant;
the fact is she did wrong. She made a mistake, as we all
do, and she now has to pay for it. The story continues
and the self-righteous crowd brings the woman to Jesus.
"They made her stand before the group." (John 8:3) So
there you are, standing in front of this group of people
who are about to kill you, because you are guilty as charged.
Jesus had bent down and started to write on the ground
with his finger.
(John 8:6) "They kept demanding an answer, so He stood
up again and said, "All right, but let the one who has
never sinned throw the first stone!" (John 8:7) Again He
stooped down and wrote on the ground. (John 8:8) "At
this, those who heard began to go away one at a time, the

older ones first, until only Jesus was left, with the woman still standing there." (John 8:9)

So, everyone has left. It's just you and Jesus standing there and He asks you, "Where are they? Has no one condemned you?" (John 8:10b)

"No one, sir," she said.

"Then neither do I condemn you," Jesus declared. "Go now and leave your life of sin." (John 8:11)

What is going through your mind right now?

Jesus has just spared your life. You were guilty, and now you're not.

No man is there to accuse you. It's as if you did nothing wrong.

What would you do now?

What would I do now? Would I celebrate my new lease on life? Would I rejoice in being saved from death? Would I feel relieved that I was no longer condemned?

Yes, I'd be thrilled, I was just spared, I was free, I was forgiven. But I still felt guilty. So what did I do? I just stood there in shock. It was too good to be true. Although I fully understood I was no longer condemned, I did not know how to receive this gift of grace and forgiveness. It was so foreign to me. So, I did not leave, but I stayed where my accusers had just been. I was completely aware that I was forgiven and no longer sentenced to death, but what did I do? I stayed right where the angry crowd had been. I stayed and began bending down to pick up all the stones my accusers had left behind!

Even though I had been cleared from all my guilt, I was going to take back all the stones of condemnation they were going to throw at me. I was going to place all the guilt back on myself! I was unable to accept that I had been forgiven because I did not feel worthy. So, I refused to let go; I was unable to forgive myself. I did not know how to receive God's grace, because I still felt guilty.

Make a Choice

This demonstrates to us that even though we experience forgiveness through Christ and come to know Him as our personal Savior, we can still hang onto the old guilt and condemnation; we got used to the stones of accusations and lies that were constantly thrown at us! We may still feel guilty, so we think that we are. But the truth is, whether we feel like it or not, we have been forgiven. We have been set free and are not longer condemned. Now it is up to us to make a choice.

Will we accept the free gift we do not deserve? Or will we hang on to our old feelings of guilt and shame?

We need to make a choice to not allow our guilty feelings to overrule the truth.

We need to make a choice to not allow our guilty feelings to overrule the truth.

- The truth is that we are forgiven, regardless of what we feel.
- The truth is that Christ liberated us and excused us from our sins, whether we feel we are worthy or not.

- The truth is that if we don't accept Christ's pardoning us, we not only hurt ourselves but we are insulting Christ because we are responding in a way that dismisses his forgiveness towards us. We are basically telling Jesus that His forgiving us was useless!

- If we don't accept this truth, we are rejecting the freedom Christ died to give us; the reason Christ came and suffered and died was in order to set us free. "It is for freedom that Christ has set us free." (Gal 5:1a)

- And in our not receiving His forgiveness, sadly, we despise His gift of freedom and love for us. We, sorrowfully, waste His grace. We act as though He did not pay the price for our forgiveness and our salvation. We, regrettably, miss the point of the mercy of God.

- And in our not receiving His gift of forgiveness toward us, we are saying that what He has done for us was not good enough. We choose to reject His goodness and kindness. And when we do this, we, sadly, despise His ultimate sacrifice for us—the laying down and forfeiting of His life—because that is what it cost Him to pay the price to clear us of our sins.

So, if we choose to not let go, we will, unfortunately, go on carrying around this load of guilt-filled rocks collected by our accusers whom Jesus sent exposed and away. We end up weighed down, with a heavy and guilt-stricken mind and heart because we refused to let go of these heavy burdens of self-guilt, self-hatred, and self-loathing.

In this verse we are warned of this: "It is for freedom that Christ has set us free. Stand firm, then, and do not let yourselves be burdened again by a yoke of slavery." (Gal 5:1a) This verse cautions us to not "take back our rocks of guilt" and not let allow ourselves be weighed down again by condemnation—the very thing Christ freed us from.

If we're not willing to let go of our guilt, we put ourselves in chains. Instead of being rich in freedom, we live as paupers of slavery. And it is totally unnecessary, because in Christ Jesus we can be free from condemnation.

How we handle our guilt also shows us how we view God. Do we believe that His laying down His own life was enough? Even if it is our own conscious that is condemning us, then we need to realize that our conscience is part of our human nature, and even our conscience needs to submit to what the word of God says!It is so sad how we suffer and struggle with anxiety, guilt-complexes, and fears because we can't let go and receive Christ's pardoning us. So we stay slaves to guilt and condemnation.

But when we, at last, let go of these stones of accusations that weigh us down, then we can be freed from the bad guilt of condemnation that causes us to be enslaved. Even if our own hearts condemn us, we let go of these rocks and put an end to our condemning ourselves.

Simply said: Since Jesus was condemned in my place, therefore there is no longer any condemnation for me.

And one by one, as we drop these stones, we enter into the wonderful life of freedom that was bought for us on the cross at Calvary.

We must make a choice to receive the truth that He has forgiven us.
As we make this choice and we choose to forgive ourselves, we can stop holding ourselves as a prisoner.

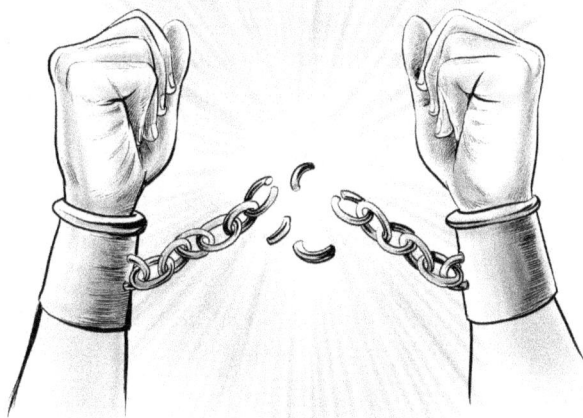

The more we embrace God's grace, the more the condemnation will fade away.

Now a change will begin to happen. The more we embrace God's grace, the more the condemnation will fade away.

Old habits, patterns of fear, shame and distrust gradually

will be transformed. You will be able to be less critical of yourself; you will be better able to lower your own expectations of yourself and others; and even be able to lower your overall expectations of this life. You will no longer dwell on the past, but with time and work, you will heal from it and move forward.

We must be mindful of choosing to see ourselves through God's eyes. Through His eyes of love, see yourself the way He does.

Through His eyes of love, see yourself the way He does.

You are no longer condemned!
Keep in mind, this healing won't happen on its own. We must "work out our salvation with fear and trembling." (Phi. 2:12a) We need "work out our salvation" in many areas of our lives, including our inner healing. Our healing requires teamwork between you and God, and many times, a trusted counselor. To "work out," in the Greek, means to continually work to bring something to completion. The "trembling" refers to a shaking due to weakness, but this weakness, our brokenness, is not a negative thing in that it serves a higher purpose of bringing us to a place where we are more dependent on God… and this, in the end, will bring us life.

Healing Is a Process
Seeing and accepting the truth, along with a willingness

to make changes, will set us on a path to freedom. But the path can be a long one; please remember to be patient with yourself!

One simple but great method to help keep your old, wrong thinking under control is to "take every thought captive to obey Christ." (2 Cor. 2:5) This spiritual strategy is a good way to begin helping your thoughts to line up with what is true and right.

We are encouraged to dwell on the things that are good: "Whatever is honorable, whatever is right, whatever is pure, whatever is lovely, whatever is of good repute, if there is any excellence and if anything worthy of praise, dwell on these things." (Phil. 4:8)

If you are taking all these steps and still seem to be plagued by condemnation, do not fret.

"Do not fret, it tends only to evil." (Ps. 37:8)

Don't give up. There is *always* hope for you!

But even if our own heart, our own conscience, or our own feelings condemn us, we can know that God is greater than our hearts. "Even if our hearts condemn us, we know that God is greater than our hearts, and He knows everything." (1 John 3:20)

We can be sure that God understands our sincerity and our dilemma, and we can be comforted in knowing that He does not condemn us even if we condemn ourselves.

Another part of growing in your freedom is for you to more fully embrace God's grace. This is a key to your living a transformed life.

Remember, forgiveness is a process, whether it entails our forgiving someone else or forgiving ourselves.

And don't be discouraged; freedom is a life-long process! Please keep this in mind: Your feelings were also wounded, so you need to allow time for your emotions to heal as well. Many times our emotions take a while to catch up with our thoughts.

Many times our emotions take a while to catch up with our thoughts.

Like the slinky dog's tail, they always seem to drag a bit behind in the healing process.

Be comforted, little by little, one by one, your emotions will catch up!

Oh, and just a quick note, it is all right to occasionally feel
sorry for yourself. On His way to the cross, Jesus spoke
to women who were crying and gave them permission
to weep for themselves. "Jesus turned and said to them,
"Daughters of Jerusalem, do not weep for me; weep for
yourselves and for your children." (Luke 23:28) There is
a time and place for self pity. Even the Lord takes pity on
us. "Then the Lord will pity his people and jealously guard
the honor of his land." (Joel 2:18a) It's ok, for a time, to
be sad for yourself. God will not despise a broken and
humbled heart.
"The sacrifice pleasing to God is a broken spirit.
You will not reject a broken and repentant heart, O God.
God, You will not despise a broken and humbled heart."
(Ps 51:17)

"Yes, Adam's one sin brings condemnation for everyone, but
Christ's one act of righteousness brings a right relationship
with God and new life for everyone." (Rom. 5:18)
It's time to begin celebrating a new life for you, today!

11

TEMPERAMENT NEEDS

God gave us many marvelous human characteristics and qualities, including personal needs. Not only did He make us with needs to be accepted and not neglected, and with needs to belong and not rejected, but He also designed each one of us with more specific needs.

God designed us with unique and specific needs.

For example, some of us have a need for more quiet time, while others need to constantly socialize. Some people need a lot of touch, hugs and affection, while others are content to keep a bit of a distance.

People are Individuals

Not everybody is the same. Some people work at a fast pace while others are slower. Some are gregarious while others don't like to work with people much at all. Some people are very easy going while others are more strong-willed. These are not characteristics that develop over time; we are born with them. As you may remember, I was being stubborn and strong-willed right from the start, while I was in the womb. (Now, looking back at that story, I wonder what in the world I was thinking… arguing and resisting the King of the Universe? Obviously, I wasn't thinking!)

It is so important that we understand our unique needs, because when our needs are met, peace is brought into our lives. When our needs are *not* met, stress is the result.

Another benefit of being aware of our needs is that when our needs are properly met these areas become our strengths, but when our needs are not met, improperly met, or ignored, these areas become our weaknesses and can result in negative and undesirable consequences in our lives. Particularly if a person has suffered abandonment or rejection, their most significant, deprived, unmet need can become this person's greatest obsession.

If a person has suffered abandonment or rejection, their most significant, deprived, unmet need can become this person's greatest obsession.

For example, if a person who has a very high need for affirmation does not receive the encouragement, praise, and recognition they deeply need, they will feel rejected and will have a tendency to become obsessive in this area, and become excessively driven to get affirmation, even in wrong ways, in order to have this need met.

Knowing Our Needs

Not only do our needs affect us and those around us, but they also affect how we relate to God. For example, if we have a high need to be in control of things, we may struggle to allow God to have control in our lives, and submitting to Him can be very frustrating. If we have a need for very little affection, we may resist opening up and establishing deep relationships with others, and do the same when it comes to our relationship with God.

Finding out your "unique temperament needs" is extremely useful to better understand yourself and how you relate to people. It can also help you in your relationship with God.

Finding out your "unique temperament needs" is extremely useful to better understand yourself and how you relate to people. It can also help you in your relationship with God.

Knowing our inner needs is also helpful in our everyday lives, because when we identify our unique needs, we can focus on finding healthy ways to meet these God-given needs.

Creation Therapy

Creation Therapy is a concept that focuses on understanding the inner man; this is referred to as the "Theory of Temperament." This theory gives us knowledge to help us understand ourselves.

The theory teaches that our temperament was placed within us by God while in our mother's womb.

God created our "inmost being." (Psalm 139:13)

Creation Therapy also teaches that we are spiritual

beings, created by God with a precise order and balance of three parts:
Body, soul, and spirit.

Our temperament was placed within us by God while in our mother's womb.

Creation Therapy is a therapeutic method that was developed in 1983 that offers a unique assessment for people desiring to know their unique "inner make-up," also referred to as "inner DNA." A person can fill out a questionnaire, consisting of scientifically derived questions. The questions are presented in such a way that children starting at the age seven can take an assessment.

The Benefits of the Assessment
Based on a scientific and mathematic methodology, the assessment results are calculated and the person's temperament is revealed. A personal report is given to the person to explain the results of the person's needs, strengths, and weaknesses, along with other helpful information. It also beneficial for the recipient to receive more details about their temperament through a clinical report available by meeting with a Certified Temperament Counselor.

The results of this assessment have a very high accuracy rate of over ninety percent, with over a thirty-year track record. It is an amazing tool recognized for its significance in helping people better understand their inborn needs. When used during counseling, the results of the report accelerate the discovery of root problems in a highly efficient manner.

If you are interested in having your own personal report to help you discover your inner identity, you can contact me via my website for more information at

www.donnaalvescounseling.com

12

ANGER

When people's emotional needs (temperament needs) go unmet, the result is often both frustration and anger. Anger is an emotion that everyone experiences. At some point we have all lost our tempers and flown off the handle out of frustration. Frustration is not to be taken lightly, since Frustration + Disappointment + Frustration = Anger. People may feel as though they are just frustrated, but it is likely that they are angry too.

Anger is one of the most volatile emotions people experience and has a high potential to do much harm.

Anger is one of the most volatile emotions and has a high potential to do much harm.

Anger Is Misunderstood

One misinterpretation about anger is that anger is always bad and we should not feel it. But anger, in itself, is not bad. It is one of our God-given emotions and it serves a purpose. Anger is a sort of built-in alarm to let us know when something isn't right. Did God say, "Do not be angry?" No. He did not. What God did say was to "Be angry... but... do not sin." We have permission to be angry, but we need to keep anger under control and not cross over the line into sin.

Sin is the point at which we hurt ourselves or hurt

someone else.

Did you know that God is angry every day? "God is an honest judge. He is angry with the wicked every day." (Psalm 7:11)

God gets angry, yet He has no sin in Him.
This assures us that anger itself is not sinful.

Anger itself is not sinful.

One way to check if we are justified in what we are angry about is to compare it with what God gets angry about. Since we are to be "imitators of God," (Eph. 5:1) we can conclude that it's ok to be mad about the things God gets mad about. We can use this standard to help measure whether we are justified in being angry. The point here is not that we have a license to be angry all the time, but rather to acknowledge that we are not to condemn ourselves for feeling angry. Nor are we being given permission to allow our anger to be like a runaway train. On the contrary, we are encouraged to, "Get rid of all bitterness, rage, anger, harsh words, and slander." (Eph. 4:31)

Anger is an emotion that has permission to be felt and expressed, but within the parameters of love.

Anger is an emotion that has permission to be felt and expressed, but within the parameters of love.

Since anger is an emotion that has the greatest tendency to lead to sin and abuse, it requires caution and is to be handled with respect, care, and proper thinking. We are to put anger aside and out of the way. "But now you also, put them all aside: anger, wrath, malice, slander, and abusive speech from your mouth." (Col. 3:8) Anger should not be what is evident in our lives, rather gentleness. "Let everyone see that you are considerate in all you do." "Let your gentleness be evident to all. The Lord is near." (Phil 4:5)

Anger Is Complex

The problem is not with anger itself, it's with how we handle it.

We often deal with anger in one of two ways:

1. We *blow up* by venting it, or

2. We *hold it in* by suppressing it.

Either way is not good. You may ask, is there a third and better way? Yes, there is. We should:

3. *Hold it back.* This means expressing anger in a controlled and thoughtful manner—not in a violent rage where it hurts others, and not stifling it where it can harm us by turning into bitterness.

Anger Is Not Always Easy to Detect

Sometimes when people experience anger it can be quite subtle. The person may just be a bit negative, sarcastic, or cynical. The person may feel some resentment, or just have a gloomy attitude, tending to be somewhat disagreeable; this can be due to anger they are holding inside.

They may not even be angry at someone else, but it could be that they are angry at themselves. This is very common for people who struggle with low self-esteem.

The undetected cycle goes like this:

Anger at self → raised expectations → failure → more anger at self.

The longer this cycle goes on, the more the person will become sad, and over time, the person can begin to feel dead inside.

An Alternative to Anger

Be sad, not mad.

It is absolutely reasonable to get mad at certain times in our lives; however, getting mad is to be something that is *occasional, not continual.*

Also, please do not misunderstand this be-sad-not-mad concept to be promoting depression; this alternative is not referring to sadness as a feeling or an emotion, but as a choice. It is what I like to refer to as a "heart posture"; it is the way we chose to carry ourselves every day.

This concept is a lifestyle of choosing to be sad and softened, rather than being mad and hardened.

Sadness is a more humble heart posture.

The beauty of being sad is that we reap the benefit of our hearts being made softer. Being softened has a benefit in that "sadness has a refining influence on us." (Eccl. 7:3b) Like how gold is melted, molded, refined, and purified by the heat of the fire, so our character is refined as we soften; the result is a beauty in our brokenness.

Anger is a more arrogant heart posture.
The consequence of being angry is that anger can make our hearts hard, which, in turn, leads to wrong and hurtful actions. Anger often carries with it feelings of being provoked and vexed, as well as resentment and exasperation. The outcome of these thoughts and emotions is that a person can become discouraged, disheartened, and lose heart. (based on Col. 3:21)

Anger does not refine us or make us more humble; to the contrary, it's detrimental in how it make us proud and arrogant, which usually leads to our doing things that God would not regard as right or righteous. The fact is that "human anger does not produce the righteousness that God desires." (James 1:20b)

It is better to be softer and humble, for "God resists the proud, but gives grace to the humble." (James 4:6b) So is it more beneficial for us to be sad than to be mad.

It is more beneficial for us to be sad than to be mad.

Anger Can Be Complicated
Anger can be complicated because it can be influenced and accumulated by many things, including people's previous life experiences, their self-image, and expectations they have of themselves.

If a situation happens in life where a person is under a higher level of pressure, this will also affect the person's level of anger.

Anger can be complicated because it can be influenced and accumulated by many things, including people's previous life experiences, their self-image, and expectations they have of themselves.

Let's take a person who is in a low-pressure environment and who's experiencing mild anger, feeling helpless, or feeling as though they have no future, particularly if they have an "I don't deserve this" mentality. Now, take them and put them in a high-pressure situation. Before, what was mild anger at self, others, at life, or at God, can flare up and turn into an extreme emotional problem. They can start to shut down, become indifferent and lethargic; they can clam up and fill up with self-pity and hopelessness. This downward spiral can reach a point where the person even despairs of life itself.

Anger can often be expressed as a mixed message. Because hurt turns into anger, anger can be pain in disguise.

Anger can often be expressed as a mixed message. Because hurt turns into anger, anger can be pain in disguise.

People respond in anger in two general ways, either by

outward hostile behavior or by inner resentment.
I would like to share this case study to illustrate an example
of outward expressions of anger.

A Very Unusual Case Study

I need to mention this was an unofficial and unusual case
study I took on as a youth. There were three reasons I
could not include this client as part of my professional
case studies:

1. The client refused to fill out his intake forms.
2. He did not show up at my office.
3. He was a cat.

This cat-client did not come to me; I had to go to him
because he was up in a tree. Not a very convenient place
for a counseling session, but we would have to find a way
to help this special client since he was obviously in a very
serious crisis.

When I first met Mittens, he was not very cooperative or
talkative, so I knew I would simply have to go by his body
language and outward expressions. This would not be too
difficult since he was meowing at the top of his lungs!

We had adopted Mittens when he was a kitten, and given
him a home. He was more social and cooperative than
the usual cat, answering to his name, sitting upon request,
and even giving his paw. On this particular day, the reason
for his being so antisocial and up in the tree was that he

had slipped off the fence and fallen into the neighbor's yard. That would not have been so bad had there not been a Siberian husky on the other side. The dog, a born hunter, instantly grabbed Mittens in the belly and bit him on his hind leg. Mittens managed to escape, and in a panic, ran up a tree. And there he sat, crying in pain. (Aw, poor thing.)

We eventually managed to get him out of the tree. We did our best to stop the bleeding as we drove him to the vet. They stitched him up, wrapped him with bandages, and sent him home. He was most attached to me, so he spent his recovery time next to my bed.

For days he sat in the corner of my room, meowing in pain both day and night. Not eating, not drinking. When I tried to give him even a few drops of water, he would howl at me. If I tried to pet him to console him he would put his ears back and hiss at me. Anything I did to try to help him, his reaction was one that told me to back off.

I did not understand, he was usually very reasonable and cooperative. Didn't he trust me?

The cat knew I was there to help him, he could see I was being so gentle, and he knew I genuinely cared about him, so why would he not let me go near him?

Exactly. Because he was in so much pain.

Days later we took him to another vet to see why he was not improving. This vet took another x-ray and found out that his hip had been dislocated. So all this while, his hip had been out of joint. (The first doctor had missed this.) The cat's leg eventually healed, but he would walk with a limp for the rest of his life.

There are several illustrations we can draw from this case study on anger.

You may be thinking that one is 'don't walk on the fence!' (Although that's a good point, that was not the main point I had in mind.)

Indirect Behavior

First real point: Because the cat was in pain, he did not want me to touch him or go near him. Have you seen this response in a person? You reach out to someone, a person who is usually very reasonable and cooperative and social, but they don't allow you to help them. Instead they react aggressively. You try to compliment someone, and all they do is disagree with you. You want to give something to someone who obviously is in need, but they refuse. They say "no" to the very thing they need, reacting polar opposite of what they really want.

This way of behavior is called *indirect behavior*. The person acts one way, when they really want the opposite. They communicate that they want you to stay away, when, actually, they are desperate for your help and want you to be close. Truthfully, they need you and want you to support them.

Are you or someone you know acting or negatively or even aggressively when people try to get close to you—physically close or possibly emotionally close to you?

If a person has inner pain, similar to how the cat was, they may act aggressively toward others. They may snap at them, answer them sharply, not make eye contact, give them short answers, or simply not open up. All these responses are ways they will try to push people away. If this doesn't work, they may escalate their intensity by yelling, having tantrums, throwing things, or retaliating by throwing insults to scare the person away. They'll do whatever it takes to get them to keep their distance, because they can't handle their pain.

The person in pain may get to the point that they won't allow anyone close enough to make them feel better—as was the case with the cat, who before had a tendency to be very social and outgoing, but because of his pain, he just wanted to be left alone!

A person may be desperate for help, but the other person might never know. All the other person sees is anger, not hurt. The worse the pain, the more extreme the person will show their anger, and the further they push people away. It's easy for other people to interpret this angry behavior in the wrong way, and see the person as completely selfish. The truth may be that the person's pain is so unbearable they are not being selfish; rather, they are helplessly self-absorbed!

And this is so sad, for by their behavior they end up scaring away the very ones who care about them and who are trying to help them.
It didn't matter that the cat knew I had his best interest in mind. It didn't matter that he knew I was there to help him. He was totally absorbed with two things, himself

and his pain.

People may be acting angrily toward you, when deep inside, their true heart's cry is that they are actually in deep pain. In their pain, they don't want anyone to help them, touch them, or even be close to them. Do you know someone like this?
Could this someone be you?

13

REJECTION

We all get hurt sometimes.

How do we respond? Do we answer gently or do we scare people off with our aggression?

How we respond will depend on many things. In particular, if a person has a history of rejection, a common way they handle their hurts is... not to. Their goal is to protect themselves. It begins with small, everyday, undetected irritations, minor frictions and pressures that slowly cause a hardness to form, little by little. Before long a callus has developed. Not outwardly on their physical skin, but in their inward emotions.

The Emotional Callus

An emotional callus is formed exactly like a natural callus; from irritation, friction and pressure. It can be a situation, a person, a hurt, or a loss.

Quietly but surely, over and over the "sore spot" is irritated. With time, the callus will become relatively thick and even hard; a direct reflection of what is happening inside the personal emotionally. Many times this happens without the person even realizing it.

Surprisingly, the purpose of a callus is a good one. It forms in order to protect a person's sensitive skin. The objective to protect one's self is good, but unfortunately, it comes with a price.

The catch is this: In order for the callus to form its protective surface, the skin has to die.

This "dying skin" is hard, thick, and dry, and has less sensitivity than normal healthy skin. As a result, the cost of an emotional callus is that the person's emotions die, taking with them the person's ability to feel, and making the person emotionally hard, thick, and dry, which may translate to their emotionally being irritable, unhappy, and depressed.

A callus itself does not hurt much. It really doesn't even bother a person too much, only under one condition: as long as the callus is left alone. However, when pressure is applied, everything changes. There is discomfort, and depending on the amount of friction and pressure, the end result is pain.

The callus that was originally intended to prevent pain, in the end, does just the opposite.

The callus that was originally intended to prevent pain, in the end, does just the opposite, leaving the person more vulnerable and susceptible to pain than they were before.

The Remedy

Removing a physical callus is very similar to removing an emotional callus. The remedy for the physical callus, is much the same as the cure for the spiritual:

Physical Remedy	Spiritual Remedy
Soaking in warm water to soften.	Being softened by love and acceptance. Coming into God's presence and receiving the warmth of His goodness.
Scrubbing with a pumice stone.	Allow people you trust and the word of God to correct and smooth.
Washing and cleaning.	Allow the truth and the Word of God to cleanse and purify.
Repeat treatment until it is gone.	Repeat treatment until it is gone.
Keep the area soft and moist.	Allow the Holy Spirit, as rain and oil do, to keep your heart soft and moist.

God Sympathizes With Us

We are not alone in our rejection, in our life's struggles, in our hurts, or in our emotional wounds.

We are not alone in our rejection, in our life's struggles, in our hurts, or in our emotional wounds.

There was a man who was:

- Despised
- Rejected and
- Forsaken by men
- A man of sorrow and suffering
- Familiar with pain
- Acquainted with grief and sickness
- One from whom men hid their faces
- His worth was not appreciated
- We had no esteem for him (Isaiah 53:3)

Do you know Him?

He too was rejected and, even today, He still continues to be rejected by many.

The world was made by Him, but the world did not know Him.

"He was in the world, and though the world was made by Him, the world did not recognize Him." (John 1:10) Jesus Himself said, "If I hadn't done such miraculous signs among them that no one else could do, they would not be guilty. But as it is, they have seen everything I did, yet they still hate Me and My Father."

But this happened so that the statement written in scripture might be fulfilled: "They hated Me for no reason." "They hated Me without a cause." (John 15:24-25)

There may be times in our lives where others may hate us without a reason.

"He is not a high priest Who cannot be touched with the feeling of our infirmities; but was in all points tempted just as we are, yet without sin." (Heb. 4:15)

He is able to sympathize with our weaknesses. "He is touched by the feelings our weaknesses." (Heb. 4:15)

He is able to sympathize with our weaknesses. He is touched by the feelings our weaknesses.

God is touched by what we feel, and can sympathize with our weaknesses. It is of great comfort that when others can only understand us to a certain degree, we can be sure that God can fully understand all of what we feel, and that "He is mindful that we are but dust." (Psalm 103:14b)

So as we go through life, we may have all sorts of difficulties, but can find comfort in knowing that we have a
God who identifies with our suffering. He knows how it
feels to hurt, to be hungry, to have no home, to be hated,
to be rejected, to be despised, beaten, betrayed, forsaken,
and condemned; and all of this without a cause.

Knowing this ushers in an assurance that "all is well"
because God knows all that hurts us and all that concerns
us. As a verse in the hymn "Blessed Assurance" written
in 1873 by Frances Crosby so simply and beautifully says,
"Perfect submission, all is at rest
I in my Savior am happy and blest
Watching and waiting, looking above
Filled with His goodness, lost in His love."
We are not alone in our struggle, in our rejection or in our
pain. With this in mind, we have strength and hope to
walk through the healing process, knowing God is with us.

God is the one who formed our hearts, and He is the one
who has seen all our heartache. He knows it all. Every bit

of it. Every minute of our suffering. So who better than
He to come to help heal it?
Remember, His love toward you is not conditional.
It is a perfect love that believes the best in you.
"His love believes all things, hopes all things, and endures
all things." (1 Cor. 13:7)
God never gives up on us, even when we give up
on ourselves.

Let the Healing Begin

So won't you make this decision… a choice for this to be
a new season in your life?
Make a decision for this to be:
- A time for you to be made new.
- A time for you to heal.
- A time for you to be comforted.
- A time for you to be made whole.

Following are eight steps to help move you in the direction
of healing:

1. Bond to God. The healing process begins by first
bonding to God, by receiving Christ as Lord and Savior
in our lives. Then we can bond in healthy ways to those
people around us.

2. Find a safe place to heal. Finding someone we can
confide in and share transparently—a trustworthy
friend, a pastor or counselor, someone with whom
we can share our heart, where we are protected and

nurtured. Also, when and if possible, do your best to remove yourself from relationships or situations that are hurtful to you over and over in the same way.

3. Know your unique needs. Learn more about your unique inner needs and focus on finding healthy ways to meet our God-given needs. To begin to love who God created us to be, and to better love ourselves.

4. Be honest. Admit our hurts, take responsibility for our feelings, and be willing to work through even those things we may, at one time, have been denying.

5. Learn to trust. Choose to trust God as well as learn to trust others.

6. Receive love. Let down our defenses, stop condemning ourselves, and allow God and others to accept us and love us.

7. Allow time. Healing is a process that happens one layer at a time. We need to be patient with ourselves as we allow God to reveal those things that need to heal.

8. Rejoice! Be thankful. Celebrate how far we have come and that our future is as bright as the sunshine, filled with His life-giving promises!

There are endless promises for each one of us as we walk through our journey of healing with God. This is one of my many favorite verses that explain how

God comes and rescues us:
"He reached down from on high and took hold of me;

He drew me out of deep waters.
He rescued me from my powerful enemy,
from my foes, who were too strong for me.

They confronted me in the day of my disaster,
but the Lord was my support.
He brought me out into a spacious place:
He rescued me because He delighted in me." (Psalm
18:16-19)

14

OUR LONGING SATISFIED

The experience I had in the womb was engrained within me and it changed my life forever... for I had been touched by God; I had tasted a drop of eternity.

Longing for More

This longing for more, this yearning for what cannot be found in this world, compelled me to seek the presence of that Someone I had once felt before. It spurred me on to find that relationship that I once knew, but had lost. It took me almost twenty years to find the One I first knew before I was born, or should I say, for Him to find me. The cold and harshness in this world caused me to forget the depth to which He cared about me. Until one day, He found me. In the midst of a cold stormy season in my adult life, I called out for Someone to save me.

The harsh waves of life were crashing over me, billows of sorrow were flooding my hope; and darkness, like a wall, on all sides, was closing in. There was nowhere else to turn; and at that crucial moment, that same Someone spoke to me.

I froze. In that moment, I became fully aware that this Someone sensed my wrestling. He could see me. And not only that, but He was aware of everything I was thinking too. He was mindful of it all.

He Again Spoke

He again spoke to me. This time it was an audible voice. He told me who He was. He spoke saying, "I am your Father, who art in heaven."

I remained still. I did not move. I knew it was Him, the One I had once known.

The same Someone I had known from the womb. At that moment in time, I reached out to Him. He rescued me. "He reached down from on high and rescued me; He drew me out of deep waters." (Psalm 18:16)

He rescued me and brought me to shore. I was tired, I was weary, I was wounded; I had a lifetime of serious emotional injuries and deep scars. But now things were different; because I knew that He was there, I had hope, and I was willing to try again.

Now, almost two decades later, I was again overwhelmed by His greatness, and His peace that passes understanding again swept over me. I again surrendered my life and my will to Him.
I now more deeply and completely chose to trust in Him. I knew, that in this life, never again would I be alone.

Now I Could Begin Again

And so my journey to freedom began. I was born anew; I had been born again. From that point forward, I knew my life would never be the same.

However, I knew that I still had many things in my life that needed to be healed. Even though I was now a "new creature" in Christ and the old was passed away, I was aware that I still had many issues to resolve, heartaches to be healed, and people to forgive.
I would now have to learn to live in a new way—how to live the right way.

We Can't Undo the Past

I could not undo the past, nor could I act as though it never happened. But I began to learn that it was possible to be set free from the past.

I learned that we could have a new identity by being a new person in Christ; that we can forgive those who

have offended us and choose to put the past behind us—acknowledging it, resolving it, and not looking back.
I came to realize that for those things that need to be healed, little by little, layer by layer, we can trust God to reveal them and then to help to heal them.

Though we cannot undo the past, it is possible to be set free from the past.

The Old Passes Away

Even though we cannot undo the past, as we move forward we will find the old thought patterns and old hurts pass away. "Therefore, if anyone is in Christ, he is a new creation. The old has passed away; behold, the new has come." (2 Cor. 5:17)

As we become more whole, our fear, rejection, condemnation, and shame start to fade away, and we can begin to live in freedom. We are able to accept the truth about our value. No longer are our identity and our joy stolen from us. His perfect love begins to drive out all our fears. "But perfect love drives out fear, because fear has to do with punishment." (1 John 4:18a) We are careful not to allow the enemy or man to tear us down. We are more alert and cautious to let no man take our crown, 'til at His feet we lay it down!
"I am coming soon. Hold on to what you have, so that no one will take your crown." (Rev 3:11)

The love of God pushes out old fears, and we no longer

feel unlovable, abandoned or worthless. And in its place, we feel significant, embraced and valued.

The love of God pushes out old fears, and we no longer feel unlovable, abandoned or worthless. And in its place, we feel significant, embraced and valued.

Learning to Trust

The losses and wounds that caused us to withdraw and distrust, slowly but surely, have less and less hold on us, and we can begin trusting others and learn to more deeply trust in God.

This trust opens the door of our hearts so we can receive the love that we so desperately need. Through our personal relationship with Jesus Christ, our love-connection with God satisfies our spiritual needs. This satisfaction overflows onto our other relationships; and now our God-given need, and longing to bond to others, can be met in healthy and satisfying ways. As we feel more safe and capable of trusting, we can allow ourselves to be more vulnerable and, as a result, gain the closeness we've been longing for with both God and others.

As we put God first, we are now motivated to love and do whatever is on our hearts, knowing that He is with us, trusting that He has our best interests in mind.

We grow deeper in our understanding of how great God

is, and begin to "grasp how wide and long and high and deep is the love of Christ." (Eph 3:18) We grow to better understand that "our present sufferings are not worthy to be compared to the glory that will be revealed to us." (Rom 8:18b)

We realize more and more that our deepest anguish and loneliest valleys are not worthy to be compared to the eternal glory that awaits us.

"For no eye has seen, nor ear heard, nor has entered into the mind of man, what God has prepared for those who love Him." (1 Cor. 2:9)

We Have Changed

We will still have our God-given needs, our desires to be fulfilled, and healthy needs we yearn to have met; and our present troubles may not go away and our circumstances may not have changed, but one thing has changed...

We have changed. We have come to better understand and more deeply know Him.

Our present troubles may not go away and our circumstances may not have changed, but one thing has changed... we have changed. We have come to better understand and more deeply know Him.

Now we have a hope and assurance of God's love and care for us; something we did not have before.

Now we can Hurt	without being Hopeless.
We can be in Anguish	without being Alone.
We can suffer Injury	but know that God Identifies with us.
And when we Cry	we are assured to be Comforted.
And with our every Pain	we can remember God's Promises to us.

As we receive His love and His promises toward us, we learn to trust God more. Now we are able trust Him, even when we have only questions and no answers.

We Trust
We trust Him when things in this life simply make no sense to us.
We come to trust His purpose and to trust His timing.
We patiently trust Him to set us free.
We lean on Him and trust Him to carry us when we are weak.
We trust Him to calm us in the midst of the storm.
We trust Him to soothe us when the pain is too hard to bear.
We learn to trust that He can repair what was broken, and restore what was stolen.

We trust Him when we can't find our way, when there is no solution, and when nobody understands.
We trust Him when our path is unseen, and the only thing we can hear is Him saying to us, "Fear not, for I am with you." (Is. 41:10)
And in the end, we learn how to more fully, and more

humbly, yield to Him.
(deep, sweet sigh)

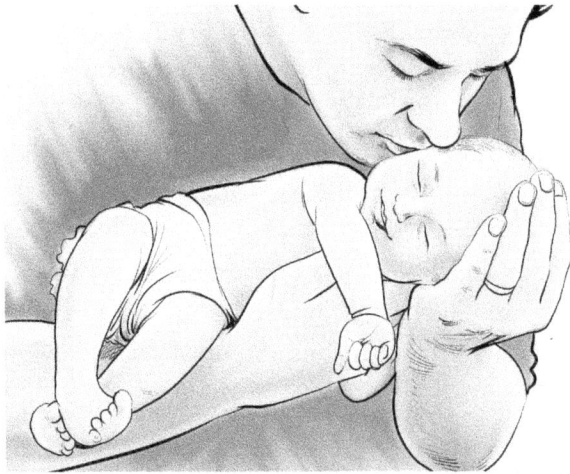

Our Deepest Longing

When I look back at that day, when it was time for me to be born, I remember how the thought of leaving the womb was so frightening. The thought of leaving the One who loved me so completely, saddened me. I did not want to leave. I did not want to go. And although, to this very day, I still deeply miss the feeling of being so close to Him… I am glad I am here.

I am glad to be here to tell you that such a perfect place exists.

To let you know that this Someone, this most gentle yet most mighty God exists, and that in His presence there is fullness of joy. There is only satisfaction, no need or wants. He Himself is the only One Who can fully satisfy the deepest longing of your heart.

So, even if you still have many unanswered questions,
Even if you are struggling with unbelief,
Even if you have hidden tears in your eyes, can you say to Him,
"God, I chose to trust You. I believe, please help my unbelief."

If you allow Him to, He will come into your life and free you,
heal you, and save you. He will change your life forever.

**For it is He who has "set eternity in our hearts."
(Eccl. 3:11b)**

**And He is the only One who can satisfy...Our Longing
For Eternity.**

www.ingramcontent.com/pod-product-compliance
Lightning Source LLC
Chambersburg PA
CBHW061945070426
42450CB00007BA/1056